GROUNDWORK GUIDES

**The Betrayal of
Africa**
Gerald Caplan
Sex for Guys
Manne Forssberg
Empire
James Laxer
Oil
James Laxer
Pornography
Debbie Nathan
Being Muslim
Haroon Siddiqui
Genocide
Jane Springer
Climate Change
Shelley Tanaka

Series Editor
Jane Springer

GROUNDWORK GUIDES

The Betrayal of Africa

Gerald Caplan

Groundwood Books
House of Anansi Press

Toronto Berkeley

Groundwood Books / House of Anansi Press
110 Spadina Avenue, Suite 801, Toronto, Ontario M5V 2K4
or c/o Publishers Group West
1700 Fourth Street, Berkeley, CA 94710

We acknowledge for their financial support of our publishing
program the Canada Council for the Arts, the Government of Canada
through the Book Publishing Industry Development Program (BPIDP)
and the Ontario Arts Council.

 ONTARIO ARTS COUNCIL
CONSEIL DES ARTS DE L'ONTARIO

Library and Archives Canada Cataloguing in Publication
Caplan, Gerald L.,
The betrayal of Africa / Gerald Caplan.
(Groundwork guides)
Includes bibliographical references and index.
ISBN-13: 978-0-88899-824-8 (bound).
ISBN-10: 0-88899-824-4 (bound).
ISBN-13: 978-0-88899-825-5 (pbk.)
ISBN-10: 0-88899-825-2 (pbk.)
1. Africa. 2. Africa–Foreign relations. I. Title. II. Series.
HN773.5.C36 2008   960   C2007-906794-8

Design by Michael Solomon
Printed and bound in Canada

Contents

1 A Diverse Continent, a Common
   Predicament   7
2 History Matters   12
3 Portrait of a Continent   37
4 The Great Conspiracy   59
5 Western Policies and Africa   83
6 The China Factor   108
7 Changing Africa   113

   Africa Timeline   129
   Notes   132
   For Further Information   135
   Acknowledgments   138
   Index   139

For Dylan and Peyton — the future

Chapter 1
A Diverse Continent, a Common Predicament

The story of Africa is literally the story of the human race. The ancestors of our species first evolved in Africa well over 3 million years ago. It's exciting to visit the University of Addis Ababa to see the wonderfully preserved skeleton of an adult female forerunner of us humans, discovered in Ethiopia in 1974; about 3.2 million years old, it's called Lucy, after a Beatles song. In 2006, the bones of a 3.3 million-year-old baby ape-girl were unearthed in Ethiopia. Her finders named her Selam, meaning "peace" in the local language, which might have been the derivation of the words *salaam* or *shalom* — peace in Arabic and Hebrew. From Selam and from Lucy eventually evolved our more direct ancestors, some of whom moved on from Africa to populate the entire world. Of course, this was so long ago that it seems to have little to do with today's world. But every person on earth can trace her or his roots back to Africa.

Africa is both a continent and a universe, or, more accurately, many mini-universes. In the days when it was still considered a primitive backwater that the white world had the right to dominate, the map of the world showed Africa to be only slightly larger than Europe. This was an outright racially motivated distortion. In fact, all of Europe could fit into Africa three times over. Africa is the second-largest and second-most populous continent after Asia. It includes five time zones, at least seven climates and, despite the one-dimensional jungle stereotypes, enormous geographical diversity. Divided into fifty-four independent countries, Africa is inhabited by some 900 million people with a wide variety of backgrounds, cultures, customs, religions, appearances and ways of life. Even skin color varies strongly, from deep black to light brown. Countries differ wildly by size. Half of all Africans live in the four countries of Nigeria, Ethiopia, the Democratic Republic of Congo (DRC) and South Africa, while many of the other half live in countries far too small to be economically viable on their own.

A good reflection of Africa's endless diversity is the existence of several thousand ethnic groups and two thousand languages. Many countries contain as many as twenty ethnic groups and languages, and some contain far more. A European language — English, French or Portuguese – is the official language, even if it's sometimes spoken only by the well-educated minority. Africans from Ghana, for example, communicate with Africans from Zambia exclusively in English, although both speak one or more local languages. One of the significant and widely recognized divisions is between the north, largely Arabic and Muslim, and the far more heterogeneous countries of sub-Saharan Africa. In a real sense, North Africa is qualitatively different from Africa

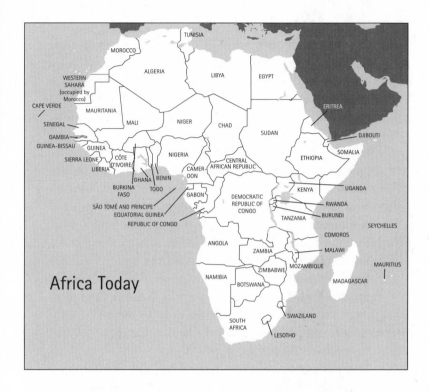

Africa Today

south of the Sahara desert, and both northerners and southerners recognize this difference. The Africa we mostly hear about is sub-Saharan Africa, and it's the forty-eight countries of that huge region of the continent that this book concerns.

But it's only possible to discuss some thing called "Africa," even sub-Saharan Africa, with great caution. Treating Africa as a single entity has been a trap for many, from nineteenth-century European imperialists to twentieth- and twenty-first-century white racists to those Africans themselves who advocate a USA — a United States of Africa. Yet despite the region's extreme complexity and diversity, and despite its many hundreds of mini-universes, a combination of factors allows us to generalize about several critical aspects of Africa today. Whatever the historical background, whatever the lingua franca, whether former colonies or not, whatever their religions, cultures, geography, climates, whether they've had self-styled Marxist rulers or free enterprisers, whether landlocked or blessed with ocean location, whether democracies or dictatorships – the overwhelming majority of sub-Saharan African countries find themselves in a remarkably similar predicament. A large number of common patterns prevail across this vast territory, responsible for much of the reality of present-day Africa. It is these shared characteristics, how they came to define the continent, and possibilities for the future that this book will investigate.

Even the uninformed outsider in the rich world is aware of the African condition: underdevelopment, conflict, famine, AIDS, wretched governance. The better-informed know that at the time of its independence in 1957, Ghana, the second African country to free itself from colonial rule, was in development terms on a par with South Korea, near the bottom of the scale. Today, the United Nations' Human Development Index ranks South Korea as 28th among 177 nations, Ghana 138th. Ghana's per capita gross domestic product is $550, South Korea's is $16,500.[1] For many, this is a vivid and accurate symbol of the African record in the past half-century.

Yet few appreciate the great constraints on Africa's present development thrown up both by unlucky geographical and climatic conditions and by Western leaders. As economist Jeffrey Sachs has noted, "Most societies with good harbors, close contact with the rich world, favorable climates, adequate energy sources, and freedom from epidemic diseases have escaped from poverty."[2] Most of Africa is not blessed with these attributes. Then, 120 years ago, European leaders, who knew nothing about African conditions and cared less, exacerbated those natural challenges when their arbitrary division of the continent created fifteen landlocked entities — another serious drawback to development.

In a multitude of ways, Africa has not been graced by either nature or humankind. These underlying constraints need to be kept in mind as we explore the challenges facing Africa today.

Chapter 2
History Matters

How do we account for Africa's plight, and what can be done about it? I think it's fair to say that the conventional wisdom, the widely accepted answers, are twofold. First, the problem is African — corruption, lack of capacity, poor leaders, eternal conflict. Second, the solution is us — by which I mean the rich, white Western world that will save Africa from itself, its leaders, its appetites, its ineptitude, its savagery.

There is in this answer more than a hint of centuries-long racist attitudes toward Africans and other black people. It's a contemporary version of the imperialist era's white man's burden. But it's hokum — arrogant, self-serving and, above all, plain wrong.

There's an alternative perspective on the "African problem," one that is not nearly as self-congratulatory and smug as the conventional wisdom. This interpretation says that rather than being the solution to Africa's plight, we Westerners are a substantial part of the problem, and have been so for centuries. None of this condones or justifies the crimes many African leaders have perpetrated against their own people. But it does help to explain the problem and to indicate the different directions that need to be taken if Africa is to find its path to a better future.

The Historical Context

When I was growing up, schools taught about the great nineteenth-century European explorers and missionaries who "discovered" Africa. David Livingstone, we learned, was the first person to discover the magnificent Victoria Falls bordering Zambia and Zimbabwe. (The closest town is now called Livingstone.) This discovery would have come as a surprise to centuries of local Africans who had always been aware of the falls, which they called Mosi-oa-Tunya — "the smoke that thunders." But so far as the world of white Europe and North America was concerned, until a white man had seen a place or a landmark, it didn't exist.

This smug distortion of history was reflected in both popular culture and intellectual discourse as recently as a few decades ago. One of the movie folk heroes in my school years was Tarzan of the African jungle — "Me Tarzan, you Jane" — whose Africa was little more than a rain forest and whose Africans were invariably subservient and subordinate. The unchallenged racism of the Tarzan films reinforced the widespread Western assumption that blacks were naturally inferior, and it profoundly shaped white stereotypes of all things African for many decades. Renowned Oxford historian Hugh Trevor-Roper excluded Africa from his course on world history on the grounds that "there is only the unrewarding gyrations of barbarous tribes in picturesque but irrelevant corners of the globe."[1] For him, African history was nothing more than the history of whites in Africa.

Western media have also played a decisive role in determining the attitude of the rich white world to Africa, often reinforcing ignorant racist stereotypes. Even the *New York Times*' prize-winning Africa correspondent in the first flush of independence during the 1960s, when all-important impressions of Africa were being forged in American minds, had little but contempt for his subjects. "Cannibalism," he wrote his editor, "may be the logical antidote to this [African] population explosion everyone talks about." The equally respected editor, in turn, welcomed the journalist as the "leading expert on sorcery, witchcraft, cannibalism and all the other exotic phenomena indigenous to darkest Africa."[2]

Racist attitudes of the media have often been encapsulated in the loaded word *tribe* or *tribal*. There are no tribes in the West; there are nations and ethnic groups. Only primitive, savage societies have tribes, although by any definition, the three main population groups of Nigeria, for example, are nations. Yet a *New York Times* story from Nigeria in 1967 referred to "small, pagan tribes dressed in leaves," which happened to be a total fabrication.[3] There were no such people in Nigeria, and the humiliating phrase was concocted by an editor sitting in New York to add color to a news story.

A little less than thirty years later, ignorant Western reporters were at it again. Somehow, Africans still didn't deserve simple human respect. In covering the early days

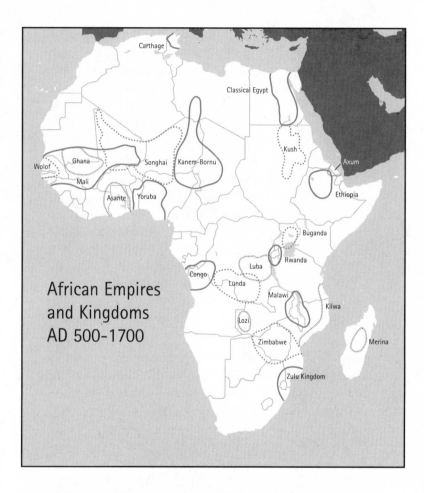

African Empires and Kingdoms AD 500–1700

Carthage

Classical Egypt

Kush

Axum

Ethiopia

Wolof

Ghana

Songhai

Kanem-Bornu

Mali

Asante

Yoruba

Buganda

Congo

Luba

Rwanda

Lunda

Malawi

Kilwa

Lozi

Zimbabwe

Merina

Zulu Kingdom

of the Rwandan genocide in 1994, most reporters, who slipped only briefly into the country, sent back stories of savage tribal warfare. The obvious conclusion was that any notion of international intervention would be a waste of time. Any sense that white Catholic missionaries and white Belgian colonial masters had been largely responsible for the terrible ethnic divisions that were haunting Rwanda, or that the genocide was a carefully organized plot by a small group of educated and sophisticated men, or that the French government was directly complicit in the genocide — all this was missing from the stories Westerners received in the early weeks of the genocide, with appalling consequences for Rwanda's targeted Tutsis. (See "The Rwandan Genocide" on pages 78-79.)

The racist stereotype of Africans as primitive savages lives on. In 2001, as he was about to head off to a conference in Mombassa, Kenya, Mel Lastman, then mayor of Toronto, Canada's largest city, asked a reporter: What the hell do I want to go to a place like Mombassa?… I'm sort of scared about going out there, but the wife is really nervous. I just see myself in a pot of boiling water with all these natives dancing around me." Was he joking, as some claimed? If so, he must have thought that this racist crack would be seen as funny. The irony is that Toronto is proud of its great diversity; it's home to some 200,000 black people, many from Africa directly or indirectly. None of these constituents found Lastman's "joke" amusing.

The persistent notion of Africa as "the dark continent," as the famous (and cruel) explorer Henry Stanley called his 1878 memoirs — dark in skin color, in obscurity, in primitivism — is a major distortion of historical reality. As a small band of experts have documented, over the millennia, and for a large part of the period before European colonial rule, sub-Saharan Africa was home to a series of great empires. Mali, Kanem-Bornu, Asante, Songhai, Zimbabwe, Axum – these were powerful empires in their time. Here is Basil Davidson, the British historian who did much to rescue Africa's remarkable history from oblivion and Western derision:

> The great lords of the Western Sudan grew famous far outside Africa for their stores of gold, their lavish gifts, their dazzling regalia and ceremonial display. When the most powerful of the emperors of Mali passed through Cairo on pilgrimage to Mecca in the fourteenth century, he ruined the price of the Egyptian gold-based dinar for several years by his presents and payments of unminted gold to courtiers and merchants.[4]

No one who has seen the underground churches of Lalibela in northern Ethiopia or the magnificent bronze and brass Ife sculptures of western Nigeria can doubt the extraordinary potential of African technology and creativity. For much of its history, Europe had little to surpass these achievements. We'll never know the outcome had Africa been permitted to develop based on its own wit and initiative, as Europe was, but of course it was allowed no such freedom. Thanks to Europe's boundless race-based self-confidence, superior technology in weaponry and shipbuilding, and the insatiable demands of its new colonies in the Americas, the European slave trade soon enveloped Africa. It is fair to say that Africa has never recovered.

Those who trace Africa's present plight back in time are often dismissed as weak-minded liberals seeking to rationalize African problems by wrapping them in the irrelevant mists of history. Yet no one would dare argue that the United States' development has not been profoundly influenced by slavery, its revolution or its civil war. Even today, books pour out by American writers on every aspect of the American Revolution and the Civil War; you could dedicate a lifetime to the task and still not be able to read even a fraction of the literature on either subject. No one claims these studies are irrelevant or that they don't address issues that matter even now. History matters, for Africa as much as for the United States, and for Africa, the slave trade and colonialism matter enormously in understanding its subsequent evolution.

The slave trade conducted by Europe ended barely 150 years ago, and in the prior 350 years an estimated 36 million to 60 million Africans were uprooted from their lands – an astonishing proportion of the continent by any standards. Estimates disagree, but perhaps 12 million to 15 million finally arrived in the New World alive. At the same time, and extending throughout the nineteenth century, Arab slavers shipped millions more Africans out of eastern Africa. It is true, as many have pointed out, that the trade couldn't have succeeded without the cooperation of Africans themselves. While Europeans already thought of themselves as the superior white race, Africans facilitating the slave trade could then hardly have thought of themselves as black people enslaving other black people. That phenomenon came in reaction to their treatment as a homogeneous race by the European interlopers.

What is beyond dispute is that African slave labor enabled the development of both the US and Europe, and ultimately crippled Africa. There is no knowing exactly how much poorer and less developed Western nations would have been without African labor or how much more advanced Africa would have been with it. But we can say confidently that economic progress in America and Europe would have been significantly stunted and that of Africa expedited. Slavery and the slave trade were not marginal activities for Europe and the Americas. For more than two centuries, as British power grew, the slave trade was the central feature of the country's foreign commerce, endorsed and profitably enjoyed by everyone from the royal family to the great landowners and merchants. In the US, cotton was king, as the expression went, and cotton plantations depended on the slave labor of African Americans. Most American presidents before the Civil War were slave owners. The labor, skills and potential of these black people were denied to their own continent, and Africa never quite recovered from this loss.

The Fruits of Colonialism

The Scramble for Africa

Hard on the heels of the slave trade came full-blown Western colonialism. Hammered and reeling from the slave trade, Africa now had to face the technological and

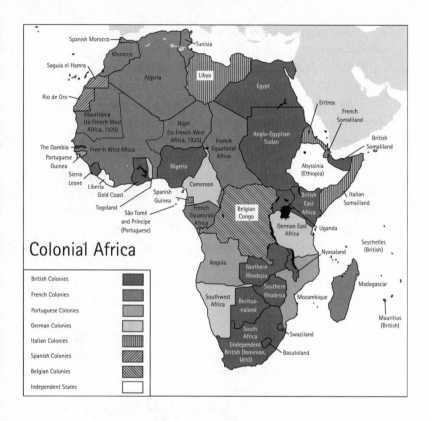

Colonial Africa

Legend	
British Colonies	
French Colonies	
Portuguese Colonies	
German Colonies	
Italian Colonies	
Spanish Colonies	
Belgian Colonies	
Independent States	

military might of a Europe driven by the competition for resources to feed its industrial revolution and justified by the conviction of its god-given racial superiority. This historic development was institutionalized with the "scramble for Africa" at the Congress of Berlin in 1884-85, which partitioned almost the entire continent among the European powers.

"We have been giving away mountains and rivers and lakes to each other," British Prime Minister Lord Salisbury admitted, "unhindered by the small impediment that we never knew exactly where they were."[5] They were unhindered as well by the fact that all these lands belonged to others. The small Central African kingdom of Rwanda, for example, was handed over to Germany by the other European powers even though no German, and indeed no white person, had ever entered it.

Decisions taken in ignorance were disastrous for Africa. The scramble created borders that cut through 177 natural ethnic or cultural groupings; probably every border in Africa divides at least one such area. Families, clans, ethnic groups and nations were all divided from one another in a purely random and arbitrary way. Alternately, families, clans, ethnic groups and nations that had had no relation with one another, or indeed that had conflicts with one another, now found themselves locked together under a new and alien governmental force.

This is not ancient history by any stretch of the imagination. The ramifications of colonialism continue to be felt in every country every day of the year. After all, South Africa — really the first European colony in Africa — has been free from white minority rule only since 1994, and until the end that one country kept almost the entire bottom 40 percent of the continent destabilized. Check the map of Africa. From Angola, Zambia and Tanzania south, no normal governance was possible while apartheid reined. Angola's civil war ended only in 2002,

Mozambique's only in 1992, Namibia won independence only in 1990, Zimbabwe only in 1980. South Africa's apartheid government was instrumental in violently destabilizing every one of them. The South African army launched raids into Lesotho, Botswana, Mozambique, Angola, Zambia and Zimbabwe. A 1989 report estimated that South Africa's destabilization operations against its neighbors inflicted a death toll of 1.5 million people and cost those countries $45 billion.[6]

Outside Southern Africa, the rest of sub-Saharan Africa has been independent for between forty and forty-five years. What that means is that every country endured colonialism for many decades longer than it's been independent. The paternalistic fashion is to rhapsodize nostalgically about the colonial era. What Africa needs, we are told by historian Niall Ferguson, is a return to the good old days of benign colonialism or liberal imperialism, with the rich white world in charge. This is a very old strategy. The wise men of Europe too were shrewd enough to disguise their greedy carving up of the continent as nothing but philanthropy. Their aim, they insisted, was instructing the "natives" and introducing them to the blessings of civilization. Some instruction. Some blessings.

In practice, nothing could be further from the truth. Colonialism by definition, and whenever necessary in practice, was based on dictatorship, violence, force, coercion, intimidation, oppression, forced taxation, exploitation, brutal reprisals and daily racial humiliation. Not a single colonial power — Germany, Britain, France,

Portugal, Belgium, Italy — is innocent of this charge. Look at King Leopold's Congo — 10 million of 20 million dead in 25 years of his personal rule. The Belgian king introduced to Africa the practice of severing hands as punishment, an abomination replicated a century later by Africans in Sierra Leone's terrible civil war. One difference was that the recent atrocities in Sierra Leone were perpetrated by a group of rebels whose "troops" included drugged-out child soldiers. In the Congo they had been carried under the order of Belgium's king, who boasted of his civilizing mission to Africa.

The list of atrocities perpetrated by Europeans is long and bloody — Belgian-like tactics emulated in the surrounding French and Portuguese colonies; the blatant theft of land by Afrikaners in South Africa and the Rhodes gang backed by Britain across Southern Africa; Britain's unilateral expropriation of the best land in Kenya; the wars of the British in the Gold Coast; the massacres by France in Madagascar; the conscription by France of their African subjects for European wars; the cruelty of the Portuguese in Angola and Mozambique; the indiscriminate slaughter of Ethiopians by Italy. It is hardly an accident of fate that the very first genocide of the twentieth century — the century of genocide, as it's now known — was by a European army, the Germans', against the Herero people of Namibia, then known as South West Africa. German settlers in the colony considered Africans to be little more than baboons and treated them in the same way; a conscious decision to exterminate an entire group of them caused little strain on the killers' consciences. The Central African Republic, a former French colony, suffered after independence under the cruel despotism of "Emperor" Jean-Bédel Bokassa. While nothing justifies Bokassa's reign of terror, it surely can't be irrelevant that when he was six years old his father, a village chief, was caned to death by a French administrator. A week after his father's murder, Bokassa's mother committed suicide from grief, leaving behind him and eleven other orphans.

In today's terms, every single European power in Africa was guilty of crimes against humanity. The kind of crimes routinely perpetrated on Africans were never considered legitimate when practiced against other whites. The rationalization that permitted such behavior was the same in every case: deep-seated racism. This attitude was perfectly reflected in the 1904 "Report of the Commissioners into the Administration of the Congo State," outlining the brutal tactics used by King Leopold of Belgium to control and exploit his personal fiefdom in the heart of Africa. After cataloguing repeated instances of treatment of the Congolese people that shocked even them, the European commissioners concluded that such behavior was necessary to rule "inferior races"and to help them up the ladder of evolution, thereby carrying out the white man's "civilizing mission."

"It is by this basis alone," they intoned, "that the Congo can enter into the pathway of modern civilization and the population be reclaimed from its natural state of barbarism."[7]

Sixty years later I heard white Rhodesians mouth the

same explanation for their dehumanization and exploitation of the white colony's Africans, the same that you could have heard from South African whites about "their" Africans thirty years after that. Judging their noble rhetoric by their actions, it was flagrant hypocrisy. Helping Africans in any way that didn't benefit whites was the very last thing all but a handful of outsiders cared about. During World War II, 374,000 Africans served in the British army, 80,000 in the French, to fight against Nazi racism on behalf of human rights that neither imperial power had the remotest intention of allowing its African subjects, including those who had fought for them.

Divide and Rule

Africa's partition by European powers was implemented with a fine disdain for existing realities. Families were separated from one another without rhyme or reason apart from the convenience of the European powers, and forced into new relationships for the same reasons. For many Africans, identifying with their new artificial colonial construct made little sense; rather than seeing themselves as Nigerian or Rwandan or Kenyan, it was more natural to reaffirm their identities as Yorubas or Hutus or Luos. Paradoxically, then, the imposition by Europe of new national entities in Africa served instead to reinforce original ties of ethnicity or clan.

In a small minority of British and French colonies, and in the two large Portuguese colonies of Angola and Mozambique, settlers were introduced to run much of the new colony. Here they created for themselves something close to a tropical paradise, certainly compared with the modest conditions most had enjoyed in Europe. White Rhodesia boasted more swimming pools per capita than anywhere on earth bar Hollywood. Virtually every family could afford a pitifully paid servant, often several. Few whites ever made a bed, washed a dish or weeded a garden. Butchers carried "boys' meat," really bones and gristle, which their "masters" bought for the servants while buying the sirloins for themselves. (This dubious legacy lives on. Any moderately successful African and all resident white expatriates have one or more servants to care for them, and most residences have servants' quarters in the back — small, cramped, with only cold water, no bath, possibly neither fridge nor stove. Whites live in a manner unimaginable except for the super-rich in their own countries, and successful Africans gain a lifestyle unattainable by most white Europeans and North Americans.)

The consequences were clear — these settler states had nothing to do with the Africans fated to live in them, and therefore little identification between them and the state resulted. It led to the kind of narrower ethnic self-identification that would plague these countries once they finally became African-ruled.

For the large majority of colonies with a handful of white administrators running the new show — only 1,300 British officials were responsible for ruling 20 million Nigerians on the eve of World War II, for example — the age-old strategy of divide and rule was implemented with a vengeance. In most colonies, under one guise or another, indirect rule prevailed. The European occupier selected a particular local "tribe" to help carry out administering the new territory, invariably causing deep resentment against this powerful chosen minority. This policy also negated the notion of loyalty to the new nation. Instead, as the end of colonial rule and the emergence of independent African governments drew nearer, the state came to be seen as an ethnic preserve rather than a national entity. Control of the state became the means to privilege for the rulers' ethnic followers and the means to oppress or ignore all others.

Africans were not merely passive victims in this process. Many tried desperately to shape their own futures. Some chose the path of armed resistance, and while they won important victories in the early years of colonialism – the Amhara in Ethiopia, the Asante, Shona and Zulu in Ghana, Rhodesia and South Africa respectively — the numerous other rebellions were all eventually overwhelmed by the superior weaponry of their Italian, British and French colonial masters. Others chose to accommodate their new rulers for very shrewd reasons of self-interest. The elite of the Lozi kingdom of the Upper Zambesi River in Zambia recognized that both the weapons carried by traders and adventurers and the Bibles carried by proselytizing missionaries were useful tools to cement their own position. They cooperated with many aspects of colonial rule, including becoming the low-level public servants who made the administration work. But no colonial ruler had any intention of sharing power with Africans. Invariably, the power of these accommodating elites was steadily whittled away. Certainly that was the Lozis' fate. In either case, then, whether resister or accommodationist, no incentive remained to feel any loyalty to the new national entity rather than to the clan or ethnic group.

This phenomenon is still widely prevalent. Although they claim to represent the nation, many political parties and even liberation movements became the instruments of specific ethnic groups. This made untenable the notion of a loyal opposition that could form a new government after winning a free election. Losing control of the instruments of the state meant losing everything under a new ethnically based government, from the capacity for corruption to actual lives. The role of government came to be seen not as developing the entire nation but as maintaining the loyalty of the rulers' faction. Political dictatorship became the form of government most appealing to ruling groups, while violent coups to usurp those dictatorships, often military-led, became the means for marginalized groups to oppose them. It also explains why so few African leaders have been prepared to step down voluntarily; if they go, so does the entire network dependent on them.

A substantial chunk of postindependence Africa's unhappy history, from the Biafran War to the Rwandan genocide, can be accounted for in this way. In other words, much of the tumult that has engulfed Africa over the past half-century has been the direct result of policies imposed on the continent by the European powers in the colonial era. To this very moment, Africa continues to suffer the consequences of those policies.

The Results of Colonial Rule

All metropolitan governments criminally neglected their colonies' welfare. Colonies had one purpose only – to serve the economic interests of the metropole or its settlers. This was not a state secret; that's what colonies were for. Whatever structures were built, whatever infrastructure developed, whatever health and schooling facilities opened, were for the good of the mother country. To their colonies these mothers showed tough love, with much toughness and little love.

Only toward the last few years of the colonial era, as the specter of independence loomed, was some small thought given to local interests. The data reveals just how small it was. In 1960, as independence was to burst upon Africa between the Sahara and Southern Africa, death rates for African children were the highest in the world, life expectancy the lowest. Only 16 percent of the population was literate, and in all of sub-Saharan Africa, with perhaps 200 million people at the time, there were 8,000 secondary school graduates. Just 3 percent of the student-age population attended secondary school. University-trained students were a rare breed. In the huge Congo, abruptly handed political independence by its Belgian masters in 1960, seventeen Congolese had a university degree. France, so proud of its colonial heritage, had not built a single university in all its colonies. More than three-quarters of both the senior public service and the managers of private businesses were foreigners.

Even as they were reluctantly giving up formal domination, the Portuguese, British and French demonstrated all that was most malign about colonialism. Portuguese settlers and officials destroyed much of Mozambique's infrastructure and buildings as they withdrew in 1975. For over thirty years, you could see the large unfinished building in the middle of the capital, Maputo, where cement had been poured into the elevator shafts to sabotage future construction. In 1960 the French carried out a similar scorched earth policy in Guinea, whose new African rulers refused postindependence cooperation with France. On their way out, French officials destroyed or carried away every desk, file and telephone in government buildings; they even pilfered the lightbulbs.

Far worse, in Madagascar in 1947, French troops killed between 90,000 and 100,000 Malagasies who were rebelling against French colonial rule; the uprising took 550 European lives. To put down an anti-British insurgency in Kenya known as Mau Mau in the 1950s, the British army killed at least 20,000 Kenyans, perhaps many more, tortured thousands, and imprisoned tens of thousands in concentration camps. Over 1,000 rebels were executed on the authorization of British-run courts, most for offenses less than murder, such as illegal possession of a gun. After four years of rebellion and white hysteria, 32 white civilians had been killed by Mau Mau fighters.

Adding up the various components of European-

Apartheid in South Africa

From the first establishment of a tiny white settlement on the southern tip of Africa in 1652, Africans were considered and treated as inferiors. In time, two distinct white groups emerged. While those of Dutch stock — the Afrikaners — and those of British background fought a long bitter battle to determine who would run the country, their views of race largely coincided. The Afrikaners were more dogmatic, convinced their particular brand of Christianity dictated white domination over savage Africans. But in practice the British were hardly less racist.

Whites and Africans lived in separate worlds except when it came to work. Whites depended on African labor, but the relationship was always deeply unequal. Blacks did the grunt work. Whites, even those who in the early years performed manual labor, were in charge. Africans accepted this relationship only under extreme duress. White brutality towards Africans was standard behavior, and a number of wars were fought between Africans and whites before white dominance was fully established.

Apartheid was the Afrikaner name for "apartness," or racial segregation. In the 1948 elections, the Nationalist Party, representing the Afrikaner "tribe," finally defeated its British rivals and formed the government. Africans, though a large majority of the population, could not vote. As the National Party had promised, it made apartheid the law of the land in every conceivable aspect of society. The country was treated as a large laboratory with the Afrikaner government playing the role of mad scientist.

The population was formally divided into racial groups — white, Bantu (black), colored (mixed race) and Asian (Asians had been brought to the country as cheap but not slave labor). The government insisted there would be separate development consistent with the best interests of all groups. Nothing could have been further from the truth. There was a distinct hierarchy of privilege, with whites at the pinnacle, blacks at the bottom and Asians and coloreds in between. Endless numbers of laws were passed, governing every facet of life, and for Africans every moment of their lives. Where you could live, whether you could vote, where you went to school, the quality of that schooling, where you could work, what jobs you could do, where you could travel, whom you could visit, whether you could own land, what public toilets you could use, what taxis and trains and buses you could use – there were laws to regulate it all. Rarely had the world seen such a systematic and deliberate attempt to implement the perfectly unequal society.

Only brute force enabled the white government to carry out its harsh policies. But no amount of suppression could end the continual resistance to apartheid and the demand for democratic rule. Over the decades, many black political groups, most notably Nelson Mandela's African National Congress, fought back using a variety of tactics. Thousands of blacks fled the country to join the resistance from abroad. They were supported by sympathetic South African whites, always a minority within the white minority. Apartheid also attracted the wrath of many elsewhere in Africa as well as in Europe and North America. The United Nations passed resolutions denouncing apartheid, economic sanctions were imposed by some Western governments, and millions of ordinary citizens in Britain, Canada and the United States refused to buy South African products.

In the 1980s, in the face of internal resistance and foreign hostility, the Afrikaner government softened certain of its segregationist policies while launching violent assaults on its political enemies both in South Africa and abroad. But it was too late for the last white-controlled island in Africa. Some Afrikaners understood they couldn't stand alone forever. South African businesses, including the powerful gold and diamond industries, were anxious to find a more stable working environment. A new President, F. W. de Klerk, believed he could reform the existing system in a way that allowed the white minority to maintain political power. He legalized all banned black political organizations and released from jail hundreds of imprisoned black leaders, most prominently Nelson Mandela, who had spent twenty-seven years in prison. The momentum undermined de Klerk's strategy. He had unleashed forces he couldn't control. In 1994, free democratic elections were held for the first time in the country's history and Mandela became the first black president. Apartheid, at long last, was formally dead.

African relations over the previous few hundred years — economic, political, industrial, military — Walter Rodney, a brilliant young historian, caught the spirit with his powerful indictment of the colonial system, summarized in the title of his 1973 book *How Europe Underdeveloped Africa*. Rodney challenged the prevailing article of faith that Africa needed Western support to move from economic and technological backwardness to Western-style modernity. He demonstrated that Europe had for centuries sucked out of Africa its resources, both human and natural, keeping it in a state of profound underdevelopment. Europe had actually *underdeveloped* Africa. Nothing in the decades since he wrote his book has contradicted the essential validity of this argument.

From Colonialism to Independence

Although few of us understood it at the time, in country after country independence was ushered in under ethnically based leaders pretending to be nationalists. The new nations faced minimal infrastructure or human capacity; a heritage of violence, authoritarianism and division; and structures that were systematically created to drain Africa's wealth and resources to the rich world. The leadership of independent Africa learned to operate within their new world with unerring skill.

What we saw, however, was something quite thrillingly different. Throughout the 1940s and 1950s, the struggle to end colonial rule spread inexorably across what was soon to be called the Third World. In the imperial homelands, progressive internationalists made the anticolonial movement one of the great causes of the mid-twentieth century and were convinced that the ending of colonialism would open a dramatic new chapter in the history of human emancipation. For these women and men, Africa especially embodied the boundless dream of a continent that would show the world how to live without the racism, violence, oppression, exploitation and inequality it had suffered for so long. Speaking to his exuberant fellow Ghanaians at the moment his country became independent in 1957, their first president and African hero, Kwame Nkrumah, declared: "Today, from now on, there is a new African in the world."[8]

Not all Westerners welcomed the new African. In 1960, a resolution at the United Nations General Assembly calling for the independence of all colonies was opposed by every European colonial power — Britain, France, Portugal, Belgium and Spain — plus the US and South Africa. But others both championed African independence and believed in the new societies it would usher in. There was just enough evidence to make the conviction credible. There was the remarkable Nkrumah himself. And anyone with the slightest interest in world affairs knew of Julius Nyerere, president of Tanzania. It said all we needed to know about this saintly man that at home he was called *Mwalimu* — "teacher." What better role model for Africa? In Zambia, Kenneth Kaunda seemed the model of personal decency who personified his creed of humanism. Above all there were the liberation movements of Southern Africa — the cause of causes for tens of millions of progressive Westerners. In

Angola, Mozambique, Rhodesia/Zimbabwe, and especially apartheid South Africa itself, Africans had discovered that peaceful protest brought only deeper oppression and launched an armed struggle to overthrow the cruel racist rule of white minorities.

For us, on the outside, these conflicts had it all — a mighty war *against* racism, privilege, oppression, inequality, a fight *for* equality, democracy, socialism, justice. Solidarity groups sprang up in every country of the Western world, thrilled to feel part of the struggle to liberate Southern Africa. We marched, we picketed, we boycotted, we met, we sang, we raised funds, we pressured. We attacked Western governments and conservative groups that supported these racist regimes. Even though the cause sometimes seemed futile, its nobility made us feel proud and honorable. Of course, it's true that hardly any of us suffered at all, or even made the slightest sacrifice besides not drinking South African wines, while the Africans on whose behalf we marched were being killed, oppressed and humiliated. Still, from our point of view at least, it was a high point in the relationship between Africa and the West.

We were fighting for the kind of Africa we always dreamt was possible. And eventually, the liberation movements we championed in every country triumphed — Zimbabwe, Mozambique, Angola, and most gloriously, South Africa. I remember the day in 1990 that Nelson Mandela was released from prison after twenty-seven years as if it were yesterday. He had been imprisoned just when I arrived in Africa for the first time, and although I participated in the anti-apartheid movement for the next quarter-century, the truth is I never expected to see him as a free man in my lifetime. So with my family, I wept shamelessly when he walked out of prison. And I could barely contain my joy when four years later, he became president in the first democratic election in South Africa's history. If you then closed your eyes and ignored the rest of Africa, if you knew nothing yet about what had begun in Rwanda that very same month, April 1994, you could remember the glorious dreams we had dreamt about a free Africa those many decades earlier.

Chapter 3
Portrait of a Continent

Many different indicators can be used to paint a comprehensive portrait of a continent as complex and diverse as Africa — life expectancy, adult literacy, levels of health and schooling, economic productivity, distribution of wealth, the status of women. On every indicator, Africa is at the bottom of the world heap, with the distance between it and all other regions growing every day.

Inequality
Let's begin with two facts that may not be widely known: Africa is not a poor continent and all Africans are not poor. Besides its fabulous natural resources, which have caused the continent far more misery than prosperity, Merrill Lynch's *2005 World Wealth Report* calculates that there are 100,000 millionaires across the continent — a mere drop in a bucket of a billion people, but a surprising number nonetheless. Their total worth is calculated at $600 billion. One-third of them live in South Africa, where their number expanded by 21 percent in 2005. Most of the new rich are black, and not a few are former freedom fighters and "comrades" in the struggle for liber-

ation from apartheid, having found the pot at the end of the rainbow nation, thanks to policies that demand some blacks share in the country's vast wealth.

Here's yet another dream shattered. Instead of at least moderate prosperity for all, many African nations now compete for the title of the most unequal places on earth. Any consultant popping in even for a brief period anywhere on the continent can see it immediately — the four- or five-star hotels they stay at (in Addis Ababa, Ethiopia, UN agencies will only board you at the four-star Hilton or the five-star Sheraton, the latter as obscene a flaunting of unrestrained opulence in the midst of unspeakable squalor as could be imagined); the completely gated and guarded "monster" homes of cabinet ministers, business people, African Union officials, UN staff and embassy officials; and the miles upon miles of jam-packed townships or slums with their tiny hovels, filthy water, open gutters, minimal sanitation, sky-high garbage mounds and nonexistent public amenities. But even the rich can't escape the broken roads, ubiquitous garbage, beggars so thick on the ground even liberals keep the windows closed in their air-conditioned SUVs, and costly Western-style restaurants and cafes without adequate sanitation facilities for customers and staff alike.

These are the external signs of the larger economic reality. To the superficial observer, much of India seems as poor and chaotic as Africa, and much of it is; yet we know that it is simultaneously a giant on an economic rampage. Africa remains mired in poverty. Of the 177 countries on UNDP's Human Development Index, the bottom 23 are all African, as are 34 of the bottom 39.

If we exclude South Africa, the continent's troubled economic powerhouse, Africa produces only as much as tiny Belgium, population 10 million. Remarkably enough, as the twenty-first century began, "the typical African economy had an income no larger than the *suburb* of a major American city."[1] What's worse, according to the UN's Economic Commission for Africa, most of these countries can't be expected to do much better because they lack the basic structures needed to develop. Historian/journalist Martin Meredith describes most African states as having become "hollowed out" after decades of mismanagement and corruption. They are, he says with utter defeatism, "no longer instruments capable of serving the public good."[2] We must hope Meredith is wrong about this, since a capable, committed government is essential for future progress. But as things stand now, the next generation of Africans will be more numerous, poorer, possibly even sicker, underemployed, less educated and more desperate than the present one.

Rural Africa

Two-thirds of all Africans live in rural areas and practice some kind of farming. In many ways, they lead very traditional lives and farm in very traditional ways. Some Westerners, after short visits to a rural community or small village, like to announce that they've seen a sight they would have seen thousands of years before — unchanging, primitive Africa. It's easy to see how they form this impression. Families may well live in mud huts, cook over a wood fire, have no electricity, running water or sanitation system. Some women may be bare-breasted while toddlers scamper around with no clothes at all. But even in the midst of such scenes from the past, change has come to rural Africa. Some change is positive, like the introduction of cell phones to enable farmers to be connected with the rest of their country and the world in a way that was only recently unimaginable. Some are far less welcome, such as the widespread presence of AIDS in many rural areas, especially in Southern Africa. Some are inevitable, such as the mass movement away from the countryside to the cities.

While rural life can be stable and comfortable, it's also true that some 70 percent of Africa's poor live in rural areas and depend predominantly on agriculture for their livelihoods.

The Women of Africa

Among the most troubling phenomenon on the continent is the situation of girls and women. It also helps to account for many of Africa's troubles.

Many African countries boast egalitarian protocols and regulations and commissions dealing with the status of women; Rwanda's Parliament has more women members than any in the world. Africa has also produced a significant number of powerhouse women who are the match of any group of peers in the world, as well as many impressive feminist NGOs. Yet the distance between this development and the reality of the overwhelming num-

The Lives of Women: Africa and the United Kingdom

Measure	Africa	UK
Female population	400 million	30 million
Life expectancy	46	80
Chance of a girl going to primary school	60%	100%
Minutes worked per day	590	413
Female literacy	53.2%	99.9%
Births attended by a midwife	43%	99%
Annual deaths in childbirth (per 100,000 population)	920	13
Women using contraception	15%	84%
Average number of children	5.5	1.7
Annual deaths during abortion	29,800	8
Women with HIV	15,000,000	21,000

Sources: United Nations Development Programme; World Bank; DFID; Commission for Africa; Save the Children; Oxfam.

ber of girls and women everywhere is vast and seemingly unbridgeable.

In fact, in many African countries women have no rights at all and are legally considered to be minors, their lives in the hands of their husbands. For them, life is brutal on every front. This includes everything from legal status to education to manual labor to social obligations to family responsibilities to AIDS to sexual victimization. At every stage, in every area, often in the name of cultural tradition — as often as not a tradition recently invented by males — women exist for the convenience of men. If it means female genital mutilation, so be it. If it means that a widow whose husband died of AIDS can be thrown out and her property forfeited to the husband's family, or that she must have sex with her brother-in-law, or that she must become one of her brother-in-law's wives, so be it. If it means that young girls are raped because urban legend claims that sex with virgins can deter or cure AIDS, so be that as well.

It's become a cliché that successful development depends, first and foremost, on liberating girls and women from their subordinate status on every front. Yet steps toward this goal are painfully, self-destructively slow. If the male leaders of Africa genuinely cared about developing their countries and reducing levels of poverty and disease, you'd think they'd make women's equality and women's liberation an absolute priority. But the data in The Lives of Women table reveal starkly what's really going on.

The Crisis of Urban Africa

Cities ought to play a key role as drivers of growth in a country's development. In Africa, they play almost the opposite role. Many African cities have grown five or even ten times larger since independence. In 1966, the population of Dar es Salaam, Tanzania's bustling capital, was about 300,000; now it's 3 million. Yet as in most other African cities, this huge influx of new settlers hasn't been matched by a growth in structures, facilities or public services like roads, houses, sewers, water systems, schools or health facilities.

Deep poverty is the fate of most city dwellers. Unemployment and underemployment are the rule rather than the exception. Vast numbers of newcomers are driven to urban areas by the harsh conditions of peasant life. Most soon become disillusioned, discovering that their only escape from chronic urban poverty is to eke out a meager living through the informal economy — spending long hours on the streets and in traffic jams selling trinkets or a pair of pants or cell-phone covers or, for the few who have the right connections, working occasionally in construction. Vastly more Africans rely on this informal and haphazard way of making a living than on the formal economy that characterizes developed countries. Few African governments give urban issues, especially urban poverty, substantial attention in their analyses or their policies, and the international institutions that profoundly influence African governments have equally failed to make it a priority.[3]

The Slums of Africa

- Seventy-two percent of all those living in cities in sub-Saharan Africa live in slums — the highest percentage in the world. This represents about 190 million people.
- Thirty-seven percent of Africans currently live in cities. By 2030 this ratio is expected to rise to more than half. This means well over 300 million slum dwellers within a quarter of a century.
- Most slum dwellers lack electricity, barely 10 percent of Africa's urban population are connected to sewers, and 80 percent have no access to running water.
- Most slum dwellers live in houses barely fit for human habitation while 40 percent live in circumstances deemed by health authorities to be life-threatening.

In the view of many, the lack of work for young Africans is a political and social time-bomb waiting to explode. Nearly two-thirds of all Africans are under twenty-five, and nearly two-thirds of them are unemployed or underemployed. In 2006 the International Labor Organization (ILO) pointed to a double whammy for young Africans: a major increase in population and a major increase in unemployment over the past decade. Another unwanted first for Africa: it's the only region in the world where the total number of young workers living on less than a dollar a day increased, from 36 million in 1995 to 45 million in 2005. The ILO report indicated that African governments were belatedly coming to realize they must find ways to "disarm this bomb." But in truth, not a single government knows where to find the tens of millions of jobs that are already needed, let alone the tens of millions more that will soon be needed.

The Unhealthy Continent

On the day after Christmas in 2004, a great tsunami – giant waves triggered by an earthquake in the Indian Ocean – overwhelmed parts of Asia and the eastern coast of Africa, killing approximately 300,000 people. It was one of the deadliest natural disasters in history, and certainly the most famous one.

Africa faces a permanent ongoing disaster almost equivalent to the 2004 tsunami every two weeks of the year, largely ignored by the rest of the world. Every week an estimated 130,000 Africans die of causes that in most cases are easily preventable. The four major killers of children are diarrhea, malaria, pneumonia and measles. Cheap, safe, available interventions exist for every one of these illnesses. Here is the extraordinary weekly breakdown of these deaths:

- AIDS   44,000
- TB   8,000
- Malaria   19,000
- Unsafe water   14,000
- Respiratory illness   18,000
- Measles and tetanus   9,500 (mostly children)
- Other   17,500

The most recent killer of Africans is AIDS. Sub-Saharan Africa, and within it Southern Africa, are more heavily affected by HIV/AIDS than any other region of the world. Some 25 million people were living with HIV at the end of 2005 while perhaps 2.7 million new infections occurred during that year. In 2006 the epidemic claimed the lives of an estimated 2 million Africans.

The worst is yet to come. In the absence of massively expanded prevention, treatment and care efforts, the AIDS toll on the continent can only rise. Its social and economic consequences are already widely felt, not only in the health sector but also in education, gender relations, industry, agriculture, transport, human resources and the economy in general. In Southern Africa especially, countries that were coming close to reaching development targets, like a decline in infant mortality or an increase in life expectancy and school enrolment, are

AIDS Is a Development Issue

- More than 60 percent of all people living with HIV (or 24.5 million) are in sub-Saharan Africa, yet the continent is home to only 12 percent of the world's population.
- Fifty-nine percent of those living with AIDS are women.
- Two million of the 24.5 million living with AIDS are children under the age of fifteen.
- Over 12 million African children have been orphaned by AIDS.
- In Africa, fewer than one in five of the millions of Africans in need of antiretroviral treatment are receiving it.

Life Expectancy at Birth in Southern Africa (male/female)

Botswana	36/35.4
Lesotho	29.6/44
Malawi	35/34.8
Mozambique	36.3/37.5
Namibia	42.9/43.8
Rwanda	36.4/40.2
South Africa	43.3/45.3
Swaziland	33.2/35.2
Tanzania	40/40.7
Uganda	41.7/43.7
Zambia	34.8/35
Zimbabwe	33.8/33.3

Female Vulnerability

Young women in many parts of Africa do not know the basic facts about AIDS. But female vulnerability stems not simply from ignorance but from pervasive disempowerment. Many women cannot exercise their right to say no to sex and are unable to negotiate condom use in their relationships.

The well-known ABC method for preventing AIDS — Abstain, Be faithful and use Condoms — has severe limits. If a female is raped, neither abstinence, faithfulness nor condoms are relevant. If a husband or boyfriend is unfaithful, abstinence is irrelevant. Few long-term couples use condoms. In fact, many women become HIV-infected through their steady partner's high-risk behaviors. Marriage therefore can actually increase a woman's HIV-risk.

Poverty has led many women and girls to sell sex in exchange for money or clothes, maybe even a cell phone. In Southern Africa, some women have felt they had no choice but to sell sex for food to feed their children.

Gender equality is urgently needed. Women must be empowered in all aspects of life, and violence against girls and women must be brought under control. All women must have, as a matter of right, legal protection against abuse and sexual violence.

Sources: Global Fund to Fight AIDS, TB and Malaria; UNAIDS; WHO; PEPFAR

finding that those targets are quickly slipping away. AIDS often strikes people in the prime of their lives. Societies begin falling apart when they lose their doctors, teachers, civil servants, police officers, not to say parents, families and communities.

The Brain Drain

The voracious plundering of Africa's precious human resources is robbing the continent of its best, brightest and most productive people. According to the

International Organization for Migration (IOM), Africa has lost one-third of its human capital, with an estimated 20,000 doctors, university lecturers, engineers and other professionals leaving the continent every year since 1990. These women and men join the 300,000 highly qualified Africans already in the diaspora, 30,000 of whom have PhDs. To fill the gap that's been left, the IOM estimates that African countries spend a remarkable $4 billion each year to employ about 100,000 non-African consultants. So rich countries benefit twice over. We get the services of trained Africans while gaining many new jobs for Westerners in Africa.

These figures include African university graduates and professionals in all fields, but the exodus is most dramatic, and has the most destructive impact, in the health field. One in four doctors and one in twenty nurses trained in Africa are now working in the thirty richest countries of the West. Yet sub-Saharan Africa is experiencing a shortage of nearly 1.5 million doctors, nurses and midwives. In its 2006 annual report, the World Health Organization (WHO) highlighted this crisis. According to its data, three-quarters of the countries in sub-Saharan Africa suffer from a severe shortage of doctors, nurses, pharmacists, lab technicians, radiographers and other health-care staff.

WHO recommends a ratio of 1 doctor per 1,000 population in order to provide a country with basic health care. As the graph opposite shows, no African country comes remotely close.

Most African doctors emigrate to Western countries.

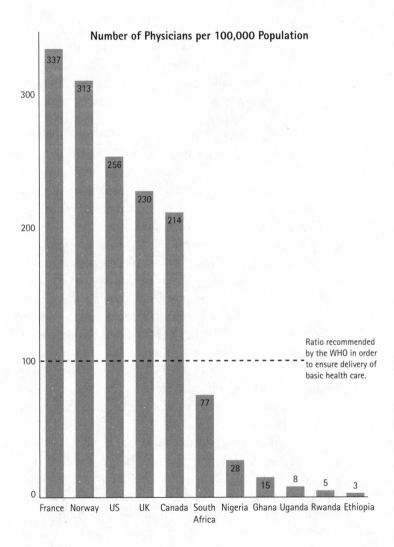

Number of Physicians per 100,000 Population

Ratio recommended by the WHO in order to ensure delivery of basic health care.

France 337
Norway 313
US 256
UK 230
Canada 214
South Africa 77
Nigeria 28
Ghana 15
Uganda 8
Rwanda 5
Ethiopia 3

More than 21,000 Nigerian doctors are practicing in the US, for example, while there is an acute shortage of physicians in Nigeria. As the graph shows, the US has almost ten times more doctors per capita than Nigeria. Large numbers also flow to South Africa, whose large First-World sector is a magnet for African professionals poorly paid elsewhere. In turn, large numbers of South Africans race off to the even brighter lights of Canada, the UK and the US, all of which have at least three times more doctors per person than South Africa. Half of all South Africa's doctors emigrate to these three countries at a huge annual cost to the country that spent so much educating and training them.

What is true for doctors is no less true for nurses. In a typical case, while the US has 773 nurses per 100,000 population, Uganda has only 6; that's 130 times fewer. The WHO sets as a minimum standard 100 nurses per 100,000 people. So the US has 7.5 times the minimum while Uganda has almost 17 times fewer than the minimum. Overall, sub-Saharan Africa needs perhaps 700,000 more health-care workers immediately, but actually loses more than it trains. That means the entire region is going backward as the need grows greater. This is no less true of those countries in Southern Africa that are being overwhelmed by HIV/AIDS. In Swaziland during 2005 and 2006, 200 nurses were trained, 150 left for the UK, and 300 more died of AIDS. Malawi has been able to fill only 28 percent of its nursing positions.

Or take Ghana, in West Africa, one of the continent's more stable and "normal" countries. Half of all

Ghanaians with college degrees live outside the country. The country is losing three-quarters of its doctors, and has lost 50 percent of its nurses to Canada, the US and Britain.[4]

According to Canada's International Development Research Centre (IDRC), poor countries in general invest about $500 million each year in training health-care professionals, who are then promptly recruited by or move to rich countries. The United States, with its 130,000 foreign physicians, has saved an estimated $26 billion in training American health-care professionals. As one Nigerian computer scientist puts it:

> We are operating one-third of African universities to satisfy the manpower needs of Great Britain and the United States. The African education budget is nothing but a supplement to the American education budget. In essence, Africa is giving developmental assistance to the wealthier western nation, which makes the rich nations richer and the poor nations poorer.[5]

The African brain drain is making a bad situation worse. But Africans can't be blamed for the problem. You can't condemn a well-trained African professional who looks for a better job abroad. That's his or her right, just as it's yours and mine. It also is an indication of exactly the kind of go-getting spirit that we in the West celebrate.

But look at the consequences for Africa. The continent's most skilled and entrepreneurial citizens have been draining away at the same time as a series of destructive economic policies were being forced on Africa by the International Monetary Fund and the World Bank. Africa cannot even begin to meet its staggering challenges, whether in health or in any other area demanding adequate skilled human resources, under these circumstances.

The State of Education

From the moment of independence, education was seen as the key that would open the door to modernization. Colonial rulers, for all their fine talk of introducing "civilization" to the unenlightened savages of Africa, initiated only the most basic schooling, usually just enough to teach a small number of Africans in each country to obey orders. That's why independent Africa placed such a great premium on universal primary education (UPE) — so that all boys and girls should go to school, and at the far end of the spectrum, on university education, where the new African elite would be produced.

A small flurry of activity followed the hoisting of the newly independent nation's flag, with large increases in the number of primary schools, many secondary schools, and at least one university in each country. But the momentum soon died out. Actual progress was replaced by a proliferation of international meetings where the need for progress was discussed. In a series of forums and summits of all kinds over past decades, both African and Western leaders solemnly vowed that UPE — now renamed EFA (Education for All) — remained the goal and that they would work together to make it happen. In virtually every country, we are still, decades and generations later, anxiously waiting.

In 2005, barely 60 percent of the children in sub-Saharan Africa went to primary school, the lowest enrolment anywhere in the world. More than 40 million African children, almost half the school-age child population, received no schooling. There were also marked gender inequalities. Two-thirds of those who get no schooling are girls. The dropout rate is also dramatic. Fewer and fewer children go each succeeding year of primary school, and secondary school enrolment is only 27 percent of boys and 21 percent of girls. The next poorest region of the world, in southern and western Asia, has double that enrolment. By university, the attrition is vast. Only 6 percent of men and 4 percent of women enroll in university, figures that are even worse for the rest of sub-Saharan Africa when you consider that South Africa enrolls close to three times that ratio.[6]

As anyone who's visited an African school can attest, just attending school is hardly the same as getting an education. With few exceptions, and especially in rural and city slum schools, students are likely to endure wildly overcrowded classrooms, few learning resources, lack of clean water and proper sanitation, no separate toilets for girls, no capacity to feed hungry children, not enough teachers, teachers who are untrained, unmotivated, badly paid, often absent, and teachers who use harsh, authoritarian methods of discipline to hammer home their teaching through memory work alone.[7]

Universities, alas, are in no better shape. In the mid-1960s, the very early years of independence, 1 percent of Africans attended university. Now the figure is closer to 6 percent. But even this statistic greatly distorts disparities among African countries, some of which barely enroll 1 percent of their students in higher education. In comparison, two-thirds of the students in rich countries go to postsecondary institutions. Where will the capacity come to govern Africa properly, to run an efficient public service, to manage state-run utilities, to become successful entrepreneurs, to fill all the professional positions required, to lead civil society in its crucial tasks? In Mozambique, to take just one glaring example, less than 3 percent of the country's public administration has received any higher education.

Africa's colonial masters built a few universities for the specific purpose of training a tiny elite that could help administer the colonies. A slew of new universities were quickly founded by the newly independent governments. Forty years on, however, with some South African universities alone excepted, virtually all African universities have fallen on hard times.

From one end of the continent to the other, we see crumbling facilities and run-down campuses, overcrowded lecture halls and hostels, depleted laboratories and libraries, computer rooms darkened by electricity cuts. Fed up by absurdly low pay and shortages of everything from books to computers, except for a dedicated minority the best African professors are escaping as quickly as they can. In Addis Ababa, the university library looks like an antiquarian bookstore and many graduates perform at perhaps senior high-school levels. There is hardly a well-stocked bookstore in most African cities. Computers and the World Wide Web are helping to introduce African students to the world missing from their universities and classrooms, but this is a long way from an advanced education guided by a well-qualified and highly motivated professor.

Two separate parties are responsible for the crisis in African education and health care — bad African leaders and poor advice from those who really controlled the major initiatives in any given African country, the International Monetary Fund (IMF) and the World Bank, supported by rich Western countries. According to the outside "experts," primary and secondary education were the priorities for economic growth, so spending on postsecondary schooling lagged far behind with the consequences that Africa is now facing. Yet as part of what they called "macroeconomic" stability, above all the need to keep inflation low, these Western-controlled financial institutions imposed limits on the levels of government spending.

These policies severely affected the entire public sector. Hiring of teachers and health-care workers had no relationship to need, however desperate. At the same time, African governments were forced to impose user fees on those attending health clinics and going to elementary school. The results were predictable, with massive falloffs of those using either public service. So while the World Bank and IMF, in a chorus with Western donor governments, loudly proclaimed their commitment to Education for All, their actual policies helped to make the goal unrealizable.

In the past few years, certain African governments have given in to pressure from their citizens to remove primary school tuitions. In Kenya, for example, even the annual $12 fee per student, which sounds insignificant to Westerners, deterred many poor families from sending their children, especially girls, to school. When President Mwai Kibaki took office in 2003, he eliminated fees up to Grade Eight. As predicted, students flooded into public schools, and, almost immediately, enrolment rose from 5.9 million to 7.6 million.

No one, however, had anticipated the impact on the quality of education. Despite the huge surge in enrolment, the Kenyan government has neither hired more teachers nor built more classrooms to deal with the increased intake. Classes now bulge with 100 students or more. Books and basic school supplies are lacking, especially in rural areas. Besieged teachers, barely trained, increasingly use outdated authoritarian methods, including widespread corporal punishment, to deal with their pupils. So while free primary education is necessary to reach out to the most vulnerable children, in practice it is stretching school systems to the breaking point in a number of countries.

Even today, having seen the consequences of their policies and claiming schooling and health to be high priorities, the IMF and World Bank continue to impose "conditionalities" that seriously limit the restoration of

Africa's health and education systems. At the same time, in Kenya the Kibaki government is accused of stealing millions of dollars that might have gone to training better teachers or building more classrooms. Once again, it appears that Africans can never win against the twin forces of Western policies and their own governments. You might well think that there's a secret conspiracy between the two to keep Africa underdeveloped. But if you look more closely, you discover that while a conspiracy indeed exists, it's not a secret to those who want to see.

Chapter 4
The Great Conspiracy

At the dawn of the independence era, both Africans and their idealistic Western friends held out great hopes for a future characterized by greater prosperity, justice and equality. Yet while independence undoubtedly opened a new stage in African history, it was hardly the one anyone had bargained for. In reality, what followed the raising of the national flag was the continuing underdevelopment of Africa.

In country after country, an implicit bargain was struck between the new ruling elites and their old oppressors among Western governments, the corporate world, and the international financial institutions controlled by the West. It is little exaggeration to describe it as a great conspiracy, and for many countries this unholy alliance has operated until this day. Instead of a commitment to reversing the policies that had so exploited and damaged the continent, the new leaders betrayed all the heady expectations they helped create. Instead of building nations that repudiated the policies and behavior of the colonial era, as the reign of the new African leaders — the "Big Men," as they were soon enough known — spread across Africa, brutality, venality and callousness followed. Africa's vast treasury of natural resources continued to pour out of the continent into the coffers of the rich world, as they had always done; soon human wealth was added to the mix. The difference now was that their former Western overlords split the plunder with their new African partners.

Both actors in the postindependence conspiracy played key roles. Part of the story of the continent's continuing crises is the betrayal by the new African elites of their own people. The other part is the role of the West. For centuries Africa's history and development had been profoundly influenced by outsiders, both Europeans and Arabs, and external influence by no means disappeared with independence. And just as most of the preindependence impact of outsiders was malign and exploitative, so has it been since colonialism ended. The rich world might have forfeited direct political control, but its power to affect the future of the continent remained as great as ever.

The fact is that we in the West are deeply complicit in every crisis bedeviling Africa, that we're up to our collective necks in retrograde practices, and that we've been virtually co-conspirators with certain African leaders in underdeveloping the continent and betraying its people. Overwhelmingly, Western activities in Africa are exploitative of the continent and destructive of its wellbeing. Where these activities have some positive aspects, as in foreign aid, their magnitude is wildly exaggerated. Contrary to our perceptions, it appears that during every year of Western interaction with Africa over the centuries, far more wealth has been drained out of Africa to the West than has been contributed to Africa. What's more, most of the horror stories associated with Africa couldn't have happened without Western complicity.

The "Big Men" of Africa

It was only a short time after Africans won formal control of their governments that Africa's Big Men began to appear. These were the leaders who became cult figures, all-powerful, answerable to no one, larger than life and rulers for life — unless violently overthrown by a rival of equal ambition and audacity. While every continent has had its share of tyrants, over the past forty years African leaders have become synonymous with tyranny — Mobutu, Idi Amin, Abacha, Bokassa, Habyarimana, Sam Doe, Charles Taylor, Mugabe, Moi, Mengistu, Habré, Bashir: the list is very, very long. It is not possible to calculate the millions of Africans murdered by their own leaders, or the amount of suffering they have caused, or the amount of money they have stolen.

Many African leaders, whether elected or not, have brought shame to their countries and continue to do so. The Nobel Prize-winning Nigerian writer Wole Soyinka reflects the humiliation felt by so many Africans who have been ruled by "a power-crazed and rapacious leadership who can only obtain their egotistical goals by oppressing the rest of us."[1] It is Africa's curse that only a handful of African rulers have been able to resist wallowing in a full-blown cult of personality.

Taking stock of the continent at the end of the 1980s, about a quarter of a century after most states outside Southern Africa became independent, historian/journalist Martin Meredith tells us that of fifty African countries, almost every one was a one-party state or a military dictatorship. Opposition parties were illegal in thirty-two of them. "Elections, when held, served mainly to confirm the incumbent president and his party in power. In 29 countries over the course of 150 elections held between 1960 and 1989, opposition parties were never allowed to win a single seat. Only three countries sustained multi-party politics, holding free elections on a regular basis." One was Senegal, another tiny Gambia, the third Botswana. For decades, Botswana stood out for being both a democracy and an economic success, until AIDS began to threaten its remarkable achievements. As well, Meredith reports, "not a single African head of state in three decades had allowed himself to be voted out of office. Of some 150 heads of state who had trodden the African stage, only six had voluntarily relinquished power." One of them had ruled for twenty years, another twenty-two years, and the third twenty-four years. Longevity of this kind soon became commonplace.[2]

Look at the records of some of the Big Men:

Jean-Bédel Bokassa, who became military dictator of the small, poverty-stricken country called the Central African Republic (CAR), had himself crowned "Emperor Bokassa I of Central Africa by the will of the Central African People." His lavish coronation in 1976 cost between $20 million and $30 million, perhaps one-third of the country's annual budget and all of France's aid to the CAR that year.

Joseph Mobutu, dictator and plunderer of Zaire/Congo, transformed himself into Mobutu Sese Seko wa za Banga, translated as "the all-powerful warrior who because of his endurance and inflexible will to win, will go from conquest to conquest leaving fire in his wake." He stole all the loans and aid that the rich world offered his country, as everyone knew he would, leaving it a hollow shell of a nation. His legacy of misrule includes the terrible wars in the Congo that broke out after he was forced to flee in 1997.

Idi Amin, the sadistic, taunting dictator of Uganda, went further than Mobutu. He became "His Excellency President for Life Field Marshal Al Hadji Dr. Idi Amin, VC, DSO, MC, King of Scotland, Lord of all the Beasts of the Earth and Fishes of the Sea and Conqueror of the British Empire in Africa in General and Uganda in Particular." His craziness was no joke, however: he was responsible for brutally murdering 300,000 of his own subjects.

In West Africa, both Guinea and Benin were transformed into so-called Marxist states. Meaningless Communist sloganeering substituted for a sound approach to the many problems both countries faced, and in the end both became poor, harsh, repressive police states, all in the name of the oppressed masses.

Look too at the record of those still in power. For years, South Africa's Thabo Mbeki and his controversial minister of health undermined serious attempts to deal

Length of Rule of Some African Presidents

Ruler	Country	Years in Power	Dates
Haile Selassie	Ethiopia	39	1930-36, 1941-74
Ahmed Sékou Touré	Guinea	26	1958-84
Hamani Diori	Niger	14	1960-74
Leopold Senghor	Senegal	20	1960-80
Ahmadu Ahidjo	Cameroon	22	1960-82
Felix Houphouët-Boigny	Côte d'Ivoire	33	1960-93
Julius Nyerere	Tanzania	24	1961-85
Jomo Kenyatta	Kenya	14	1964-78
Kenneth Kaunda	Zambia	27	1964-91
Hastings Banda	Malawi	30	1964-94
Joseph Mobuto	Congo/Zaire	32	1965-97
Jean-Bédel Bokassa	CAR	13	1966-79
Omar Bongo	Gabon	39 and counting	1967-
Gnassingbé Eyadéma	Togo	38	1967-2005
Gaafar Numeiry	Sudan	16	1969-85
Juvénal Habyarimana	Rwanda	21	1973-94
Mengistu Haile Mariam	Ethiopia	14	1977-91
Daniel arap Moi	Kenya	24	1978-2002
José Eduardo dos Santos	Angola	27 and counting	1979-
Robert Mugabe	Zimbabwe	26 and counting	1980-
Jerry Rawlings	Ghana	20	1981-2001
Paul Biya	Cameroon	24 and counting	1982-
Lansana Conté	Guinea	22 and counting	1984-
Yoweri Museveni	Uganda	20 and counting	1986-
Joaquim Chissano	Mozambique	19	1986-2005
Omar al-Bashir	Sudan	17 and counting	1989-
Sam Nujoma	Namibia	15	1990-2005
Nelson Mandela	South Africa	5	1994-99

with one of the world's greatest AIDS crises; it is unknown how many hundreds of thousands of South African citizens died before Mbeki was humiliated enough on the international stage to reverse his deadly obstructionism.

Zimbabwe's Robert Mugabe has so flagrantly devastated his country and tyrannized his people that he has brought the entire continent into disrepute. Zimbabwe was a country with excellent prospects after it won a hard-fought struggle for independence in 1980 against the white minority. But Mugabe's intolerance of opposition and the brutal and irrational policies he introduced have transformed the breadbasket of Africa into a full-blown basket case.

In Swaziland, a tiny poverty-stricken nation with the world's second-largest HIV prevalence rate of 34 percent, Africa's only absolute monarch allows no opposition parties, has taken thirteen wives (many teenagers), built them ten palaces and bought them ten BMWs, and bought himself a Daimler Chrysler Maybach 62, one of the world's most expensive cars.

In Malawi, number 165 of 175 on the United Nations Human Development Index, the newly elected "reform" president Bingu wa Mutharika chose the huge legislative building for his official residence, bought a Maybach like the King of Swaziland, and commissioned an official portrait to be painted at a cost of $800,000. The president also put his vice-president on trial for treason, accused of conspiring to assassinate him. The vice-president says he is being persecuted because he refused to join the new political party Mr. Mutharika formed after he was elected in 2004.

In Uganda, President Museveni, long a favorite of Western governments, who's been head of state since 1986, changed the constitution so he could run for a third time. He too has had his leading opponent charged with treason, but added the charge of rape as well.

Former President Obasanjo of Nigeria, a self-declared democrat, similarly maneuvered for a constitutional change so he could run for a third term. He failed, apparently being outbribed by his opponents.

Gabon's president Omar Bongo, who has held office since 1967, in January 2006 secured another seven-year term in his oil-rich and desperately poor Central African country.

In some ways, this record is not surprising. After all, being head of an African country is a pretty good job, if you are one of the lucky ones who wasn't either assassinated or overthrown, imprisoned and tortured. Most who survived became very rich, blithely equating the wealth of their country with their own possessions. Family members, cabinet ministers, judges and other senior officials and close friends weren't far behind.

When there are so many examples, it's inevitable that they're seen not as isolated cases but as a reflection of the entire continent. They have been the rule, not the exception. Who can resist thinking: *This* is Africa?

Conflict

Big Men beget conflict. They provoke fights. Whether

against other countries or against internal forces, fighting, conflict and war have been the norm for much of Africa ever since the independence victories of the early 1960s.

Between 1960 and 2004, twenty-six wars were fought and nearly 200 coups attempted. There were eighty violent or unconstitutional changes of government. Half of all the presidents in office were overthrown. At least twenty-five heads of government were killed in political violence. Governments were overthrown in thirty-one countries, in twenty of them more than once. Violent regime change led in most cases to the wide-scale murder of former officials and the emergence of even worse governments.

More recently, this record has been improving. In early 2007, there were perhaps six or seven "active" conflicts in sub-Saharan Africa. Only five years earlier, by contrast, there was a peak of sixteen. In 2002, one in three sub-Saharan African countries was experiencing war of some kind.

But it's too early to cheer this welcome news. Conflict — latent, active or recent — continues to bedevil large parts of the continent. In January 2007, Ethiopia suddenly invaded Somalia. Concerned that Somalia was harboring anti-American terrorists, the United States had persuaded the Ethiopian government to attack. Like all such conflicts, the consequences were unpredictable. After a brief period of stability, once again Somalia faces anarchy and violence and Ethiopian troops remain in the country. The resumption of war between Ethiopia and

Eritrea, largely for reasons of national pride, is also a possibility.

Far away in West Africa, in February 2007, a state of emergency was declared in Guinea by President Lansana Conté, a Big Man who has ruled his country since 1984; riots broke out across the country and police and army retaliated brutally.

In Africa, failed or ruined or non-states are commonplace. These are states with no government or with a government that has no capacity to govern. Angola, Liberia, Burundi, Sierra Leone, the Central African Republic, southern Sudan and Congo-Brazzaville are all emerging, slowly and precariously, from internal fighting. The challenges each faces even to reach a "normal" level of African underdevelopment border on the intractable. It's better to be a "postconflict state" dealing with post-conflict reconstruction than to be in the midst of actual war. But no one should underestimate the monumental problems created by the chaos, devastation and trauma of conflict or the lack of human and financial resources to meet them.

Conflicts of varying degrees of destructiveness continue in Côte d'Ivoire, in western Sudan (Darfur), between Sudan and Chad, in Chad, in the Central African Republic, in northern Uganda with the Lord's Resistance Army and throughout the vast Democratic Republic of Congo (sometimes aided and abetted by Rwanda and Uganda). Forty turbulent years after independence, Nigeria, one of Africa's linchpin states, remains its "open sore," in the words of famed writer Wole Soyinka. The country is in a continual state of imminent implosion; internal conflicts pit against one another religions, regions, political factions, ethnic groups, villages and economic classes.

Across Southern Africa the spread of HIV/AIDS threatens the very existence of Lesotho, Swaziland and Zambia, according to the leaders of these countries. AIDS is also undermining the success of Botswana, while South Africa, whose well-being is decisive to Africa's future, has proportionally more HIV/AIDS sufferers than anywhere else on earth, with fully 5 million of its citizens infected with the virus. Some believe the widespread criminal violence in these countries reflects a society destabilized by the disease.

The Role of Outsiders

In almost every case of egregious African governance, you can be sure to find Western influences playing a central role. Hardly a single Big Man would have been able to attain power, or remain in office, without the active support of one or another Western government, primarily the US and France, with Britain and Belgium in the game as well. This remains true to some extent even today. And few of the conflicts that have ravaged the continent would have been sustainable without the active intervention of Western governments, including the US, France, Portugal, Britain and Belgium. For decades the continent was seen by the West, above all by the US, as a major battleground where Cold War rivalries were played out, though the USSR played only a comparatively modest role.

The most significant intervention by the Soviet Union

African Tyrants and Their Friends

- South African apartheid was backed by the US and British governments.
- Ian Smith's white-ruled Rhodesia (Zimbabwe) was actively supported by British interests.
- In Angola and Mozambique, the US came in behind Portugal and South Africa to train and arm rebel groups that opposed the leftist African governments.
- Belgium and the US worked with Congo secessionists and Belgian mine-owners to murder Patrice Lumumba, the Congo's first and only democratically elected president.
- The US and the World Bank actively propped up Zaire's Joseph Mobuto, known by many as "America's tyrant."
- In Uganda, the British backed Idi Amin against his predecessor's "socialist" policies.
- France propped up an array of tinpot tyrants in all its fourteen-odd sub-Saharan Africa Francophone former colonies.
- The US supported military dictators in Somalia and Chad.
- The Rwandan genocide was enabled by the ethnic divisions fomented by the Catholic Church and the Belgian governments; was executed with the complicity of the French government; and was successful because of the refusal of the US government to intervene (see pages 78-80).

was in training and providing arms to many Southern African liberation movements. In context, this must be seen as a positive contribution while Western governments were backing the white racist regimes in South Africa, Southern Rhodesia (Zimbabwe), Northern Rhodesia (Zambia), Angola and Mozambique. But the Soviet record was hardly spotless. The USSR also provided arms on an opportunistic basis in various other conflicts, while its most reckless moment came when it intervened, together with Cuba, with massive military might in Ethiopia in the late 1970s. The goal was to prop up the so-called Marxist military regime that had taken

- Oil companies grow fat on the oil of the Nigerian delta, while the local people go without lights, clean water and jobs.
- In Sudan, the US supported an Islamist military dictator for many years, and now colludes with that country's government in the "war on terrorism," although the US accuses it of orchestrating a genocide in Darfur, western Sudan.
- Oil companies happily share their loot with the same Sudanese genocidal government.
- China buys Sudanese oil and refuses to pressure its government to stop the killings in Darfur, while also welcoming dictators like Zimbabwe's Mugabe.
- Mugabe's tyranny is also bolstered by three British-based financial institutions, which have together provided more than $1 billion in direct and indirect funding: Barclays Bank, Standard Chartered Bank and the insurance firm Old Mutual. Their economic lifeline keeps Mugabe's regime afloat.
- US and British governments embrace Uganda's Museveni, regardless of his changes to the constitution to hold his place in power and his failure to stop the depredations of the Lord's Resistance Army.

power by force in Ethiopia, for seventeen years one of the most violent and murderous governments on the continent. Once again, in the name of socialist solidarity and a better world, Communist regimes were responsible for terror and death on an almost unimaginable level.

It's not possible to overemphasize the pain the Big Men caused the citizens they should have been helping and protecting. But they never operated in isolation or without powerful foreign backing. The Central African Republic was a former French colony and France supported Bokassa until close to the end of his cruel reign. French president Giscard d'Estaing was a personal friend and loyal supporter who supplied Bokassa's government with financial and military backing. In exchange, France received uranium, vital for its nuclear weapons program, while Giscard and friends were taken on luxurious hunting trips and the French president was given frequent gifts of diamonds for his own use. Every part of the intimate French-CAR relationship was dirty.

The Mobutu case is similar, possibly even more flagrant. Unlike the CAR, the Congo is one of Africa's most important countries and Mobutu was among its remarkable characters. Mobutu's road to power was facilitated by the murder of Patrice Lumumba, the first elected Congolese president, which was ordered by President Dwight Eisenhower, planned by the American CIA and the Belgians, and carried out by the Belgians and some Congolese allies. A biography of Mobutu by American Sean Kelly was titled *America's Tyrant: The CIA and Mobutu of Zaire*. So his record as a despot and one of Africa's greatest thieves isn't exactly a secret. Yet the US, France and Belgium (the Congo's former colonial master) all lavished aid on him, while the IMF and World Bank gave him multiple loans worth hundreds of millions of dollars. All the donors knew that he would steal whatever they gave to build another fantastic palace or buy another fleet of luxury cars (for a country with no roads to speak of) or hide the money away in a Swiss bank account. Of course you couldn't do a single one of these things without the cooperation of foreign businesses and Western governments.

All this was in the noble name of anti-Communism

and the need to maintain a stable Zaire (as Mobutu renamed the Congo) so that its unparalleled natural resources wouldn't be prey to some far-fetched socialist revolution. Instead of being warned to clean up his act or forfeit his multimillion-dollar payoffs, Mobutu was treated to remarkable tributes. On a visit to Zaire's capital of Kinshasa in 1982, George Bush Sr., then Ronald Reagan's vice-president, told Mobutu that he had "come to respect your dedication to fairness and reason. I have come to admire, Mr. President, your personal courage and leadership." When Mobutu visited Washington, Bush described him as "one of [America's] most valued friends. And we are proud and very, very pleased to have you here today."[3] No wonder Mobutu and other Big Men were confident they could get away with anything. They could, and they did.

Some African Big Men were not heads of their countries, so they tried to undermine and overthrow existing governments, in the process causing mass death and misery. One of the most notorious was Jonas Savimbi, an Angolan who led a long rebellion that laid Angola waste. Once Angola won its independence from Portugal, Savimbi's insatiable ambition led him to launch a vicious rebellion against its leftist government lasting almost thirty years and ending only in 2002, when he was killed in a shoot-out with government troops. Thanks mostly to Savimbi, 500,000 Angolans were killed or died from disease and malnutrition.

But because the Angolan government called itself Marxist and was supported by the USSR, Savimbi became a pet of the American administration, which gave his UNITA rebel movement anti-aircraft and anti-tank missiles, and of American conservatives, who swooned over him on his many triumphal trips to Washington. Dick Cheney, then chief of staff to President Gerald Ford, now George W. Bush's vice-president and one of the architects of the US invasion of Iraq, was a prominent Savimbi champion. The Heritage Foundation, a Washington propaganda institution dedicated to extreme conservative causes and an adviser to President Reagan, also took Savimbi under its wing, considering him a great "freedom-fighter." Jeane Kirkpatrick, Reagan's ambassador to the United Nations, called Savimbi "one of the few authentic heroes of our time."[4]

The cynical twist here was that American conservatives have been singularly uninterested in the well-being of African Americans, let alone of Africans. Savimbi also worked closely with South Africa's apartheid government, even though its members explicitly considered all Africans to be inferior creatures. Under Ronald Reagan's presidency, the US worked closely with South African intelligence services against "Communists" — that is, any African who wanted a democratic government in South Africa, like the imprisoned Nelson Mandela. Both the US and South Africa worked jointly on behalf of Savimbi and his cause. Somehow, the anti-Communist cause took priority over the ruination of the Angolan economy and the deaths of half a million people. As Henry Kissinger acknowledged, the issue was America's credibility in the world; Angolans had to be sacrificed so that some other hypothetical villain elsewhere would learn not to challenge the United States.[5] As with so much of the horror inflicted on Africa with the support of the rich world, Africans were mere pawns in the agendas of foreign powers, and their interests always came last.

Except perhaps for AIDS, Africa's most deadly and intractable crisis is the conflict that has consumed the Democratic Republic of Congo (DRC) for the past seven years. As many as 4 million Congolese have died in this time, some murdered, most the victims of war-induced disease and hunger. This low-level war has claimed more lives than any armed conflict since World War II. It is true that the governments of Rwanda and Uganda have at various stages been deeply involved in this morass. But it is equally true that at the root of the crisis is US support for Congo/Zaire's late president Mobutu over a thirty-year period. Beyond that, during the 1994 Rwandan genocide, the French army in Rwanda allowed unrepentant Hutu genocidaires to flee into the DRC, where they re-grouped to continue their genocidal "work," virtually guaranteeing a military response from the new Tutsi-led government of Rwanda.

At the same time, mineral extraction companies, largely unpublicized and with the blessings of government officials, continue to plunder the Congo's resources as they do in so much of the continent. The theft of the Congo's natural riches has been dubbed "organized crime perpetrated through multi-national businesses."[6] A 2005 Human Rights Watch report, "The Curse of Gold," identified Ugandan officials and multinational corporations that were using local rebel militias to smuggle gold out of the Congo. The Western companies that were cited included high-profile giant mining corporations based in South Africa and Sweden, which in turn are partnered with other resource extraction companies based in the UK and Canada.

The boards of these companies are chock-a-block with the Western world's political elites and retired politicians who are household names. All, of course, deny involvement in illicit activities, and the Western media have proven singularly uninterested in mentioning their names or in pursuing the accusations against them. As a result, most people in the West know nothing about this issue. Yet all of us Westerners benefit from the resources being plundered; the companies enrich themselves and local Congolese officials, and the exploitation of some of the world's most miserable people continues. It is as pure an example of the Great Conspiracy as can be imagined.

Corruption

Corruption in Africa is often identified as the greatest single cause of the continent's poverty and underdevelopment. That's not true. As this book demonstrates, there are a number of reasons that explain the state of the continent. Nevertheless, the corruption so widely associated with Africa is no exaggeration. Direct bribery can extend from the elites (for a government contract) to the principal (to get into school), the teacher (for better grades), the civil servant (for a passport), the tax official (to avoid paying taxes), the doctor (for an appointment), the airline agent (for a seat) and the cop (for a phony traffic violation). Police, civil servants and teachers often demand bribes in order to make ends meet on their meager salaries; the rich just want to get richer.

According to a 2002 African Union report, African elites steal $148 billion a year from their fellow citizens; that's more than a quarter of the continent's entire gross domestic product. Transparency International's 2006 Corruption Perception Index (an imperfect but telling source) reports that of 163 countries tallied, 5 of the worst 10 and 20 of the worst 40 are in sub-Saharan Africa. In the 1990s, Kenya's ex-president Moi and his political and business pals stole more than a billion dollars in only one of their endless scams. The money they took would have been enough to pay for universal primary education in the country for a decade. The World Bank calculates that Nigerian leaders have stolen $300 billion in oil revenues in the past forty years, while 75 percent of the population lives on less than a dollar a day.

The Role of Outsiders
But the other side of the equation is usually overlooked. It takes two to tango. It would be quite impossible to steal the hundreds of billions involved without extensive outside collusion. Much of the vast amount of money accumulated by African leaders has been given to them as bribes by Western businesses, while Western governments and banks have generously provided indispensable help in sneaking the loot out of the continent. This has not been merely an altruistic operation, however; private

The Rwandan Genocide

The Rwandan genocide was one of the seminal events of the twentieth century, in a perverse way the appropriate culmination to what many genocide specialists call the Century of Genocide. But it was more than a peculiarly grisly 100 days in the life of humanity. The entire history of Rwanda in the century leading up to and including the genocide is a perfect example of the Great Conspiracy between Western and African elites that cost ordinary Rwandans so much loss and pain and caused so many deaths with consequences for the whole of Central Africa.

While there were distinguishable groups called Hutus and Tutsis before the colonial era, these distinctions were sharpened and institutionalized early in the twentieth century by Christian missionaries working with the European colonizing power, first Germany, then Belgium. The Belgians issued identity cards bearing people's ethnic group. Before independence, based on divisive racist myths invented by Catholic priests, the Belgians embraced the Tutsis, whom they saw as marching haltingly toward the exalted heights of white people like themselves. Though the Tutsis numbered no more than 15 percent of the population, the Belgians created a small privileged elite among the Tutsis to help them govern the country, with the Hutu majority treated as little better than serfs. But the time was soon ripe for de-colonization and majority rule (not the same as democracy by any means). By the late 1950s and early 1960s, Hutu leaders demanded, and won, Rwanda's independence, but not before several unprecedented anti-Tutsi pogroms led to many deaths and large-scale refugee movements into neighboring countries.

Over the next thirty years, under two different administrations, the country was effectively ruled by Hutu military dictatorships, legitimized by the enthusiastic support of the churches, with strict quotas imposed on Tutsis in both schools and jobs. For a good chunk of this period, there was little communal violence in the country and anti-Tutsi propaganda was low-key. Outside the country, however, Tutsi refugees demanded, with no success, the right of return. Finally, the conflict-generated refugees led to a refugee-generated conflict. In 1990, the predominantly Tutsi Rwandan Patriotic Front (RPF) invaded Rwanda from Uganda. The Habyarimana government had the choice of mobilizing all

Rwandans in a nationalist crusade against these foreign aggressors, or mobilizing all Hutus in an ethnic crusade against the RPF and all the Tutsis in the country. They cynically chose the latter, from which all subsequent events flowed.

Aided by French troops, the government fought the English-speaking RPF to a standstill for the next three and a half years. A series of massacres of Tutsis, the first in seventeen years, were warning signs of potential catastrophe. With the end of the Cold War, Habyarimana was pressured by outside powers to agree to a new government, sharing significant power with the RPF. The signing of the Arusha agreement in 1993 proved the last straw for the Hutu Power extremists, who surrounded the president and his ambitious first lady. With the economy also in freefall, they concluded that the only way to hang on to their privileges was to eliminate the entire Tutsi population; publicly they insisted the nation could only be purified by the total annihilation of these dehumanized aliens or "cockroaches." With an air of doom increasingly pervading the country, the UN dispatched a small, inadequate military mission, UNAMIR (United Nations Assistance Mission for Rwanda), commanded by General Roméo Dallaire. Although devoid of any African experience and given the benefit of no briefing whatever, Dallaire quickly grasped that the situation was cataclysmic. For the next six months, his constant warnings and pleas to his UN superiors in New York for reinforcements from the international community were ignored.

Just before 8:30 p.m. on April 6, 1994, a private jet carrying President Habyarimana and the president of next-door Burundi to Kigali was blown out of the sky. Logic says the deed was organized by Hutu extremists, afraid the president was selling them out. Genocide deniers and others with a mixed bag of motives have always accused the RPF. They may be right. The truth is no one knows, and no investigation into the crash has ever been undertaken — itself one of the great untold stories of our time. What we do know is that the president's death was the trigger that launched the genocide.

Over the next 100 days, in a carefully coordinated assault organized from the very top of the Rwandan Hutu hierarchy, at least 600,000 and perhaps closer to a million Tutsis were slaughtered, many in the most gruesome ways possible.

Thousands of moderate Hutus, opponents of the government, were systematically hunted down and murdered as well. Much research remains to be done on all aspects of the genocide, but it appears that of a total Hutu population of 6 million to 7 million, several hundred thousand probably took part in the killing and millions more were involved in less direct ways.

For three years prior to the genocide, the French had worked hand-in-glove with the top echelons of both the Rwandan government and the military. They knew that terrible deeds were being carried out by their allies and said nothing about them. They also knew that even worse deeds were being planned but did nothing to prevent those either. The case that France was complicit in the genocide is very strong, except that it's unlikely that the French, any more than anyone else, really believed that a full-blown genocide was imminent; at the time the concept still seemed largely unthinkable. But the French, under socialist President François Mitterrand, were certainly guilty of complicity in mass murder and ethnic atrocities. However, like the Catholic Church, which also played a deplorable role in the genocide, the French disclaim the slightest responsibility for the events of April to July 1994 and refuse to make the slightest apology.

During the genocide, it was the United States' turn to lead the betrayal of Rwanda. Having lost eighteen Rangers on the streets of Mogadishu, Somalia, only six months earlier — portrayed in the book and movie *Black Hawk Down* — the Clinton administration, under pressure from the Republicans, energetically ensured that the UN Security Council would do nothing to beef up Roméo Dallaire's puny force. Two weeks into the genocide, with tens of thousands of Tutsis known to have been killed, the Security Council considered a motion to withdraw the Rwandan mission entirely; instead, too ashamed to go quite that far, they slashed it from 4,500 to 270 troops. Many weeks later, as the reality of the genocide unfolded, the Council finally agreed to bolster Dallaire's force. But thanks entirely to American stalling tactics, by the time the RPF defeated the genocidaire government and ended the genocide after 100 days, not a single reinforcement of soldier or weapon had reached Rwanda.

Even today, it all seems impossible to believe — unless you've heard of Darfur.

firms have been major beneficiaries of stolen money and other assets spirited out of Africa. Without Western bribes and without Western assistance in laundering the money, big-time African corruption would be dramatically less significant than it is. It would simply be impossible for Africans to steal the quantities involved without outside help. In fact, such bribes are just one component of what Patrick Smith, editor of London's *Africa Confidential* magazine, calls "a system run by an international network of criminals: from the corrupt bankers in London and Geneva who launder the money; the lawyers and accountants in London and Paris who set up the front companies and trusts to collect the bribes or 'commissions'; the contract-hungry Western company directors who offer the bribes and pocket some for themselves."[7]

While the world hears unending stories of African corruption, we hear less about what's stolen by Western corporations or of the indispensable role in the corruption racket played by Western governments. Through a combination of tax avoidance and capital flight, according to African Union research, an estimated $150 billion is in effect stolen from Africa every year by foreign companies. Combined with what African elites steal, that's a loss of almost $300 billion a year. That's an astounding amount of money for the continent to lose. It seems that almost one-third of sub-Saharan Africa's annual gross domestic product (GDP) is moved from Africa to secretive tax havens that have been set up by Western governments and banks.[8] It can hardly be an accident that despite their mountains of research into so many aspects of African life, neither the World Bank nor the IMF have ever investigated issues of capital flight and tax avoidance by corporations. But the Bank has estimated that 40 percent of Africa's private wealth is held in the offshore havens created by Western governments and banks.

While most corrupt Africans are restricted to looting their own country alone, those Westerners in the system described by Patrick Smith are likely facilitating mass thievery from several different countries at the same time. That's why creative friends of Africa are considering setting up a counter to Transparency International, which might see, for example, Switzerland or France or the US or the UK ranked in the top ten corrupt countries instead of the usual African suspects. The new organization would be kept busy 24/7 delving into ways Western governments and businesses facilitate the plunder of Africa. There are a thousand places it could begin its work. Tax havens would be one.[9]

The collective complicity of Western governments and banks, multinational corporations and African business and political leaders in this massive fraud is a perfect example of the great conspiracy against the people of the continent.

Chapter 5
Western Policies and Africa

Far from being Africa's savior, we have seen that Western leaders have conspired with the worst of their African counterparts to perpetuate tyrannical regimes, plunder the continent's resources, and facilitate the criminal activities of corrupt officials and businesspeople. But there are other areas critical to Africa's development, chiefly economic and social policies, which are mostly controlled by the West. Why foreigners should have such influence over whether Africa progresses or not, whether poverty and disparities in wealth are reduced, whether more babies and their mothers live or die, whether more girls get proper schooling, whether a farmer can make a living, whether men practice safe sex and minimize the threat of AIDS — why all these crucial matters are in the hands of outsiders is simply a reflection of the way the world works today, like it or not. Those with power and wealth determine how things will be for those without.

Western influence in Africa is effected through many arrangements. Here are nine of the most important:

national sovereignty; neoliberalism; debt; investment; trade; faith-based policies; the environment; health research and drug prices; and aid.

National Sovereignty

Mighty debates are held about the propriety and legality of armed intervention by a state or states against another state. Diplomats and government officials fret endlessly about violating sovereign jurisdictions by intervening militarily in conflict situations; that's one of the excuses for allowing the atrocities in Darfur, organized by the government of Sudan, to continue. Yet not a single African country has the sovereign right to introduce policies that would shape its own destiny. African governments must either implement the policies laid down by the Western-controlled international financial institutions, above all the International Monetary Fund (IMF) and the World Bank together with Western governments, or forfeit future aid, loans, debt relief and general international acceptance. Words such as neocolonialism — economic control of a poor country by a rich one without formal power — are out of favor, and imperialism has recently been magically transformed into a benign concept, in the face of all the contrary evidence. In fact, both are alive and well and living in Africa, much to the detriment of Africa's people.

Here's the assessment of Jeffrey Sachs, one of the US's celebrity economists:

The IMF routinely works with the finance ministers of impoverished countries to set budget ceilings on health, education, water, sanitation, agricultural infrastructure and other basic needs, in the full knowledge that the consequence is mass suffering and death which would be avoided with more aid… The aid shortfall results in a human catastrophe, with deaths from hunger, disease and unsafe water on the scale of a world war.[1]

This is a most remarkable charge by a man with an international reputation who knows his financial institutions well. Isn't he explicitly accusing a leading Western institution, supported by the world's rich governments, of mass murder? Sachs's view is shared by practitioners in the field. As a prominent Zambian pediatrician told me, for him IMF will always stand for the Infant Mortality Fund.

Neocolonialism is also the precise term to describe the relations between France and its former colonies. France made sure that almost all the fourteen newly independent countries after 1960 depended on French economic subsidies, presidential aides, military advisers and civil servants to make the machinery of government work. Frenchmen dominated industry, banking and trade as completely after independence as before. French troops were stationed permanently in several African countries, either to support rulers the French approved of or to help make way for more cooperative figureheads. Just as the United States has for two centuries regarded Latin America as its backyard, to dominate as it chooses, so

French Africa was regarded, quite explicitly, as France's private estate, where other Western powers were out of bounds. France's support for the French-speaking Hutu genocidal government of Rwanda in the early 1990s was largely driven by hatred for English-speaking Tutsi Rwandans who had rebelled in order to gain a share of power.

Neoliberalism

Countless books and reports have been written about the failure of the kind of "market fundamentalism" (to use the phrase coined by Nobel Prize-winner Joseph Stiglitz[2]) unilaterally imposed on Africa and all poor countries over the past twenty-five years. In order to achieve something called "the macroeconomic health" of poor countries, it was necessary to impose "conditionalities" in return for loans and aid. In other words, the loans came with strings attached and a lot of fine print. As Jeffrey Sachs puts it, the prescription dictated by the IMF and World Bank has been "budgetary belt-tightening for patients much too poor to own belts"; the consequence has been "the collapse of public services."[3]

Conditionalities demanded by the international financial institutions (IFIs) typically included the standard one-size-fits-all prescriptions of privatization, limited government, government austerity, fees for crucial public services, and trade liberalization. Some call it "root-canal economics" because it's so painful for the average African. So instead of improving the effectiveness of public water utilities, in country after country they were privatized and foreign corporations were free to increase water costs for the poorest people on earth. Subsidies for such basics as cooking oil were removed, so these same people had to pay much more just to cook their single meal a day of crushed corn. While in all rich countries primary and secondary education is free and in most health care is a public cost, the poorest countries were forced to introduce fees for schooling and health clinics.

Called the Washington Consensus or Structural Adjustment Programs (SAPs), these policies have overwhelmingly failed to grow African economies. They have succeeded magnificently in increasing poverty and the gap between rich and poor, both between Africa and the rich world and within African countries. (The backlash, in the form of electing progressive governments, is now being felt all across Latin America, where years of SAPs have met with generally miserable results.) When these facts became so blatant that even their authors at the World Bank and IMF could no longer deny them, when it became politically correct to care deeply about poverty, the economic geniuses simply tacked the words "poverty reduction" on all their old programs and carried on with business as usual. Now we have Poverty Reduction Strategy Papers (PRSPs to development insiders) as fig leaves for the same old discredited right-wing nostrums. Having failed so often, the Bank and IMF still believed that the only sensible road was to impose the same policies over and over again in the hope that maybe one day they would work — if the country in question was still functioning.

Debt

The enormous debts that African governments owe to Western governments and financial institutions have gained a great deal of attention in the past few years. Unfair debts became a rallying cry of civil society groups in every Western country and across Africa, where governments were pleased that the issue had gained such a high profile. The more money poor governments must allocate to debt repayment, the less they have to spend on food, clean water, housing, health care, jobs, education and building infrastructure.

So successful was this campaign that debt relief for Africa became the centerpiece of the annual G8 Summit of Western leaders in 2005 at Gleneagles in the United Kingdom. Impressive-sounding commitments to reduce Africa's debt were loudly made. After the TV cameras left, the West did forgive some of the debts of some African governments, so they no longer have to repay them. But the amounts forgiven are far less than Western politicians like to boast about, and the debt burden that remains is still crushing many poor countries.

There are two issues to clarify here, one of them rarely ever raised. First, much of what Africa owes to the West ought properly to be considered "odious" debts. That means they should be considered illegitimate and should not have to be repaid. They are the result of loans advanced enthusiastically and often at extremely high rates by Western financiers to the many tyrants and dictators who have ruled Africa with Western support. Yet not even in the case of Rwanda, where the $1-billion debt was incurred by a government largely responsible for the 1994 genocide, or of South Africa, which inherited a debt of $22 billion from its apartheid predecessor, is there discussion of canceling these odious debts. This has not been the case for Iraq, where George W. Bush called for the cancellation of the debt incurred under Saddam Hussein. Yet in some sixteen African countries, a case can be made that the debt inherited from dictators is legally odious.

Second, beyond this issue of justice, the debts accumulated by almost all African governments have led to an enormous outflow of scarce capital from Africa to the West — a direct reverse transfer from the poorest of the poor to the richest of the rich.

Here's a list of the most outrageous debts left behind by some of Africa's Western-backed tyrants:

Country	Billions of US Dollars
Nigeria	$30
South Africa	$22
DRC	$13
Sudan	$9
Ethiopia	$8
Kenya	$5.8
Congo	$4.5
Mali	$2.5
Somalia	$2.3
Malawi	$2.2
Togo	$1.4
Liberia	$1.2
Rwanda	$1
Uganda	$0.6

This phenomenon has been exceedingly well documented. According to the UN Conference on Trade and Development (UNCTAD), between 1970 and 2002, sub-Saharan Africa received $294 billion in loans, paid out $268 billion in debt service, and yet still owes $300 billion.

For all the heart-wrenching pledges of Western leaders to forgive Africa's debts if (as always) certain conditions are met, the reality is often the exact opposite of what it seems. Take the so-called debt cancellation deal imposed on Nigeria in 2005. On paper it was one of the largest such operations ever, with $18 billion, 60 percent of Nigeria's outstanding debt, written off. But any celebration ignores one small detail: one of the poorest countries on earth is obligated to pay upfront another $12.5 billion of its debt to some of the richest banks and governments in the world. This represents a huge percentage of all the aid Nigeria will receive for years to come. What's more, most of the country's debt is odious, as it was incurred by military dictatorships. Even more unfairly, calculations around debt repayment are based on Nigeria's great oil wealth, not on the needs of a country where more than 80 million people live on less than $1 a day. Everyone knows that while oil companies and many Nigerian politicians have benefited enormously from oil revenues, Nigeria's citizens have benefited little. Yet the West crows about this deal as if Nigeria's development problems will soon be a thing of the past.[4]

The consequences for individual African countries — those at the very bottom of the development index, after all — have also been extensively documented, and they are breathtaking. A few examples of a widespread phenomenon tell the story: Zambia spends half of its yearly national budget repaying its debt. Ethiopia spends $6 per capita repaying its debt, $2.50 per capita on education. Mozambique, Niger and Uganda all spend more on debt repayment than on health and education combined.

In other words, instead of congratulating ourselves for our generous loans to needy African countries, we need to see how the terms for repaying those loans are another way Westerners are jeopardizing critical health and education programs while greatly enriching themselves in the process.

Investment

For many years, mainstream economists and development consultants have insisted that foreign direct investment (FDI) is the answer to Africa's prayers. According to this thinking, what Africa needs is private capital in large amounts that would transform African economies into thriving capitalist economies. This proposition has always been fraudulent. It ignores the central role that governments have played, along with private capital, in the development of every Western country. Moreover, it holds out a hope that's utterly delusional in any foreseeable timeline. It would be far more useful to draw attention to the massive flight of capital out of Africa and to determine how it can be halted.

First, Africa gets only a tiny fraction of the world's FDI, a statistic that hasn't changed for years.

Second, the overwhelming percentage of FDI has always gone to a small number of countries, usually those with significant oil reserves and other extractive industries, plus South Africa. Ninety percent of all US FDI in Africa, for example, goes to extractive industries — oil, minerals (gold, diamond, coltan, platinum) and timber. According to a 2006 UNCTAD report, foreign direct investment in Africa hit a record $31 billion in 2005, a rise of 78 percent from the year before. But the bulk of the money was poured into the oil, gas and mining sectors because of rampant commodity prices, resulting in limited gains for the poor in those countries.

Third, the very term *investment* badly distorts what's really going on. Plundering, looting and exploiting the nonrenewable resources of Africa is a far more accurate description. Consider the case of the many communities in Nigeria's oil-rich Delta region, where most people live in mud huts. Some reside only a few feet away from the oil wells that are worth billions to the giant oil companies and millions to Nigerian politicians. Yet most of the Delta's inhabitants lack electricity, indoor toilets and running water and have no hospitals or schools. They often don't even have jobs because the giant foreign-owned oil companies bring in foreign workers for even the most menial tasks. What they do have is serious environmental damage, including useless farmland and barren rivers.

Fourth, in the large majority of cases, the foreign company pays few taxes or none at all, increases corruption by bribing its way to its objectives, builds no lasting infrastructure to leave behind, pays starvation wages, destabilizes communities, uses private militias for security and becomes involved in (and may be partly responsible for) local conflicts, then disappears, leaving an environmental and social disaster behind. There are innumerable case studies from mines, oil wells and forests throughout the continent that document the way foreign companies shortchange the treasuries of the countries they work in.

As it stands now, FDI, instead of being Africa's salvation, is yet another of Africa's curses.

Trade

One of the key policies that poor countries have had imposed on them is free trade, a demand that all markets be open to one another's trade. This move is promoted as virtually a guarantee of rapid economic growth. But one might well say of free trade what Gandhi said when asked what he thought of Western civilization. It sounds like a good idea, he responded; they should try it one day.

When it comes to rich and poor countries, so-called free trade is a one-way street. As any meeting of the World Trade Organization (WTO) demonstrates, Africa is forced to play by the trade rules dictated by Western governments, who have the real power within the WTO. African countries are obliged to open their markets to Western products, but the West ignores its reciprocal obligations at will. The European Union and the US spend $1 billion a day in subsidies to agriculture, mainly large agribusinesses. Japan and South Korea also generously subsidize their farmers. This allows rich countries to flood Africa with commodities at lower prices than African producers can match, while rich countries' protectionist policies make it difficult for the products of poor countries to gain a market foothold in Western markets.

Even where trade rules are equivalent for rich and poor countries, the enormous differences in their economies ensure that one side benefits far more than the other. When the international financial institutions (IFIs) force a poor country to open its markets, almost invariably its imports from rich countries rise far faster than its exports to rich countries. The costs to the poor are immediate. Producers from poor countries can't compete with highly subsidized Western agribusinesses.

According to a 2006 study by Christian Aid, sub-Saharan Africa is $272 billion worse off thanks to free trade policies forced on it by the West as a condition of receiving aid, loans and debt relief. This is the income these countries have lost in the past twenty years as they were obligated to open their markets to cheap imports, destroying local industries. Had they not been required to liberalize, sub-Saharan African countries would have had enough extra income to wipe out their debts and have sufficient left over to pay for every child to be vaccinated and go to school. Two decades of liberalization has cost sub-Saharan Africa roughly what it has received in aid. Really this aid did no more than compensate African countries for the losses they sustained by meeting the harsh "conditionalities" that were attached to it.

An example of this phenomenon is the poultry business. Thanks to subsidies by the US and European governments, it became cheaper for a West African to buy a chicken imported from Europe than to buy one from a neighbor who was raising them. Ghanaian farmers' share of the domestic chicken market shrank from 95 percent in 1992 to just over 10 percent a decade later. Hundreds of thousands of jobs in the poultry business across West Africa have been lost or are jeopardized as Western sales of chicken in poor countries expands.

Cotton, vital for much of West and Central Africa, is another crop in great jeopardy. Cotton is the livelihood of 10 million to 15 million people in Burkina Faso, Benin, Cameroon, the Central African Republic, Chad, Côte d'Ivoire, Ghana, Guinea, Mali, Niger, Nigeria, Senegal and Togo. At the December 2005 WTO meeting in Hong Kong, African representatives made it clear to the US and Europe that their subsidies to their cotton growers threaten the livelihoods of up to 15 million people in West and Central Africa who depend on "white gold." African cotton growers carefully spelled out for the WTO how "Cotton allows us to send our children to school, care for our health and buy agricultural tools, which allow us to have enough to eat and to produce enough cereal stocks."

But these realities were no match for the powerful and highly organized cotton lobby in the United States. Between 1999 and 2003, American legislators agreed to subsidize US cotton to the tune of $12.47 billion, three times the entire budget of USAID, the American government development agency. The move led to staggering losses for producers in West and Central Africa. The IMF and UNCTAD agree that African countries have seen $250 million in direct losses and $1 billion in indirect losses.

"Some years ago, cotton for us was a source of wealth," says Malian President Amadou Toumani Touré (ATT, to all and sundry). "But these days it has become our burden, a cause of poverty."[5] Toure is one of Africa's "good guys," a professional soldier who gained the presidency of his country in a coup but voluntarily resigned, until some years later when he ran and won a fair election. Western leaders swear up and down that good governance will bring African states their due reward. Tell that to ATT and his fellow leaders.

Faith-based Policies

Under President George Bush, the US has increased its spending on AIDS in Africa. Yet it has taken other steps that undermine many of the advances that the AIDS funds have enabled. So-called faith-based policies promoted by the American government are in fact exacerbating a number of crucial health problems in Africa and other poor countries, including reproductive health and AIDS prevention programs. The US stands alone in denying funding for family planning or other sexual and reproductive health services to any agency that fails to repudiate abortions. Although President Bush's own investigators have confirmed that the UN Population Fund (UNFPA) does not support abortions, the president insists it does and he has refused to hand over funds that Congress approved for the agency.

The fact that UNFPA has been denied at least $160 million during Bush's presidency so far means that critical family planning and contraception programs all over the world have been seriously set back. South Africa, which has one of the world's worst AIDS crises, has legalized abortion, so it's ineligible to have its sexual and reproductive health programs funded. Three of the five family planning facilities supported by the International Planned Parenthood Federation in Kenya have been forced to close their doors. UNFPA and the organizations it supports offer supplies and health care that allow the poorest women on earth access to contraception, prenatal care and safe childbirth. UNFPA calculates that the money President Bush has denied them could have helped prevent up to 10 million unwanted pregnancies and 23,000 maternal deaths in poor countries, while saving the lives of close to 400,000 newborns.

In yet another faith-based policy, the Bush administration spends large amounts of money promoting sexual abstinence among Africans. The popular ABC concept of AIDS prevention — Abstain, Be faithful, use Condoms — has been transformed by George Bush into an Anything But Condoms proposition. This means that the single most potentially successful way to prevent the spread of the virus — using condoms — is being undermined.

Abstaining from sex is not an easy sell in any society. In many African countries, large numbers of girls and women, perhaps a majority, have little power and can't exercise their right to refuse to have sex. Often a wife is infected by her husband who is sleeping with more than one woman. Violent sexual assaults against girls and women are another way the HIV virus is transmitted, and females can do nothing to prevent this. Yet the Bush abstinence policy takes little account of these realities. Faith trumps reality and common sense. In April 2006, the medical journal *The Lancet* published an editorial describing Bush's approach to prevention as "ill-informed and ideologically driven." It called for "a complete reversal of policy... Many more lives will be saved if condom use is promoted heavily alongside messages to abstain and be faithful."[6] To date, the US government has paid no attention.

American policies also demand that projects receiving US funding must not work cooperatively with sex workers to promote safe sex. Yet every authority in the field recognizes that safe sex among sex workers is a key means of AIDS prevention.

With American aid funds widely available for projects that conform to President Bush's religious-based policies, many NGOs and church groups, both in the US and Africa, have eagerly come forward to jump on the anti-ABC bandwagon. They support the latest American attack on solutions based on research and oppose practical and effective means of AIDS prevention. We can only guesstimate the magnitude of the damage done, but it is surely considerable.

The Environment

Most of the world's scientists believe global warming is leading to severe climate changes with possibly catastrophic effects. The cause is the largely uncontrolled emission of carbon dioxide and other greenhouse gases by rich countries, above all the US, and by some newly developing countries, especially China, the second-biggest emitter of carbon dioxide in the world. Africa, because it has so little industry, contributes less than 3 percent of the global emissions of carbon dioxide. Yet as usual, Africa may end up paying the greatest penalty for the rich world's gluttony as well as for China's refusal to

How Climate Change Might Affect Africa

- Rising temperatures, less drinking water, increased frequency and severity of droughts and floods, and rising sea levels will severely set back progress in all areas of development.
- Dramatic declines in rainfall could cause a fall in crop yields and catastrophic famines.
- Heat waves will bring increased health problems and death.
- Desertification could accelerate around the Sahara, causing mass migrations of populations, almost all of them very poor.
- Severe water shortages will be common.
- Diseases such as malaria, dengue fever and cholera may increase; millions more Africans could be at risk of malaria epidemics.
- Christian Aid, a British-based charity, estimates that up to 182 million people in sub-Saharan Africa could die of diseases directly attributable to climate change by the end of this century.
- Decreases in the amount of arable land, land for grazing cattle, drinkable water and firewood will lead to more conflicts, such as the one now devastating the Darfur region of Sudan.

take global warming seriously. The most recent research on climate change evokes a nightmare scenario for Africa in the not too distant future.

Even when the impact of global warming might seem to be welcome, it proves not to be. Some areas of Africa will get wetter, but this may not be the expected good news for drought-hit areas such as Ethiopia. For them, wetter weather is likely to mean storms and floods and even greater soil erosion. Climate unpredictability makes life difficult for subsistence farmers, who remain the majority in most African countries. A 2006 report points out that the average number of food emergencies in Africa per year has almost tripled since the mid-1980s.[7]

Outside forces have other devastating impacts on the African environment. According to the World Wildlife Foundation, two-thirds of the forests in the Congo River basin could disappear within fifty years if logging and mineral exploitation continue at present rates. In fact, there are fears that the World Bank, in the name of economic growth, working together with international corporations, is pushing weak or rapacious African governments to allow even more aggressive plundering of the continent's precious resources with little compensation to the public sphere. As Bank officials are well aware, the government of the Democratic Republic of Congo has already signed a number of questionable deals with foreign mining and logging companies, giving away many millions, if not billions, of dollars' worth of copper and cobalt with minimal if any returns to the state. No doubt senior Congo officials have benefited substantially, and the companies expect to get very rich from this windfall. Apparently neither the environment nor the people of the Congo are factors to be considered.

Health Research and Drug Prices
Anyone working in the international health field knows about the 90:10 — 10:90 rule. It's very simple: Ninety percent of the research by drug companies targets the health problems of 10 percent of the world's population, namely citizens of the rich world. Ten percent of health

research is directed toward those with 90 percent of the world's "global burden of disease," that is, most of the conditions that affect a majority of the world's poor citizens.

The research focus has nothing whatever to do with public health or alleviating the conditions of those most in need. It's simply what makes the most money for those doing the research. Some diseases with few sufferers are highly researched, presumably because high prices can be charged for the final product. At the same time, many health problems with what scientists call "a high burden," that is, with many sufferers, are poorly researched. There is still no reliable antiretroviral drug for children with AIDS — a calamity for African families. On the other hand, for most of human history, yellow teeth or male balding have not been seen as critical health issues. Yet these new-found "conditions" now attract far more research funding than many of the common diseases that afflict tens of millions of Africans.

To make matters worse, when drugs useful to Africa are developed, they're often unaffordable. The notion of so-called intellectual property rights — a significant contradiction of otherwise sacred Western capitalist principles of free trade and free markets — has led the major pharmaceutical companies to charge inflated prices for drugs that are cheap to make and desperately needed. The commercial rights of one of the world's most lucrative industries trump the human rights of those who urgently need affordable medicine. On behalf of Big Pharma (as the drug giants are called), with their generous political donations and intense lobbying of politicians, the US and EU continue to try to force African governments to accept major constraints on the use of cheaper generic drugs through a series of individually negotiated trade agreements. It's very hard for African countries to say no when US negotiators put on the pressure.

Aid or Official Development Assistance (ODA)

Foreign aid is the connection between rich and poor worlds that most Westerners are aware of. Yet almost everything the majority believes about aid is wrong. What's more, Westerners of good faith disagree passionately with one another about the utility of foreign aid. To oversimplify their polarized positions, some believe all aid going through untrustworthy governments is wasted and should cease completely. Others believe the problem is that Western governments are contributing substantially less aid than they should. In certain ways both camps are right, but the issues aren't easily resolved.

The real story behind foreign aid is not that it has exploited Africa, as is the case with all the other issues mentioned here. The real story is how much less real aid there's been than almost everyone believes. First, although it's not often remembered these days, donor aid to Africa dropped 40 percent during the 1990s, as the West's Cold War victory made it less necessary to buy the loyalty of African governments. Though the quantity of aid has picked up since 2000, it has not yet reached earlier totals.

Second, most of us have accepted official aid figures

too uncritically. As a result, even liberally minded Westerners have bemoaned the many billions of aid dollars that have flooded into Africa over the past forty years — several Marshall Plans, as it's been vividly described — with precious little to show for it. Recent research, however, has demonstrated the pathetic reality behind the official numbers. It's often difficult, for example, to determine what really constitutes ODA in any country's budget. Debt relief, for instance, is often lumped in as a form of aid. As well, some countries still receive aid money for their political connections to the big donors rather than for developmental purposes, yet those figures too get lumped in with more conventionally understood forms of aid. Westerners should click on their countries' aid websites — USAID and CIDA, respectively, for the US and Canada — and see how much sense they can make of what they find there.

Much aid is still "tied," as it has been since the notion of rich countries aiding poor ones was introduced nearly a half-century ago. That means that whatever it does for the poor country, which is often unclear, aid always directly benefits the rich country's commerce. Let's use Canada as an example. As recently as the 2003 budget, somewhere between half and two-thirds of all "foreign aid" was tied to the purchase of Canadian goods and services, even if this made little sense in terms of costs or efficiency. As the 2005 [Tony] Blair Commission on Africa acknowledged, only a small proportion of all aid is actually not tied, with Italy and the US being the worst offenders. OECD research has concluded that seventy cents of every dollar of US aid is spent on American goods and services. Virtually all American food aid dollars (even for emergency food) is spent on American food and is shipped on American vessels; this is good for American farmers and American shipowners, but it dramatically reduces the amount of food that can be bought with limited funds and prolongs the time it takes to reach Africa.

Tied aid is but one manifestation of a larger category that's come to be known as "phantom aid." This is "aid" that really has nothing to do with development assistance as it's normally understood, let alone with reducing poverty, the supposed goal of aid programs. As defined by the British NGO Action Aid, it includes:

> Failure to target aid at the poorest countries, runaway spending on overpriced technical assistance from international consultants, tying aid to purchases from donor countries' own firms, cumbersome and ill-coordinated planning, implementation, monitoring and reporting requirements, excessive administrative costs, late and partial disbursements, double counting of debt relief, and aid spending on immigration services.[8]

All of these factors greatly deflate the real value of aid figures. A too-typical study of technical assistance in Mozambique, for example, found that rich countries were spending $350 million on "technical assistants," meaning well-paid consultants from rich countries, while the entire wage bill for the country's public service —

every single department — was $74 million.[9] In another revealing case, a US Congressional study found that for most ODA-granting countries, a large portion of apparent aid never leaves the country of origin at all. The report estimates that at least 60 percent of supposed American aid funding is spent within the US. Action Aid research claims that up to 90 percent of both US and French aid is phantom aid, and that 60 percent of all aid flows are phantom. The Blair Commission also indicated that France and the US are the major phantom donors. Some Western government officials challenge the accuracy of these harsh and embarrassing data. But no one in the aid business can doubt that the analysis is fundamentally valid.

For decades the rich world has repeatedly pledged to provide .7 percent of GNP in ODA. Yet with the honorable exceptions of four small northern European states — Sweden, Norway, Denmark and Holland — this solemn commitment is a cruel hoax. Not a single one of the large European countries or Canada or the US comes even close. Collectively, the G8 countries — Canada, the US, the UK, France, Germany, Italy, Japan and Russia — may be spending as little as .07 on real aid, ten times less than the target. Yet surveys show, for example, that a majority of Americans believe that up to a quarter of the country's entire budget goes to foreign aid, a huge sum in the range of $750 billion; in reality it's closer to one-fiftieth of 1 percent of that budget. As it happens, the US has given a far smaller proportion of GNP to ODA than any other rich nation (though Italy has now replaced it). George W. Bush has increased the amount from .1 percent to about .15 percent of GNP, which amounts in theory to $3 billion a year for Africa — a trivial amount when divided up among fifty-odd countries. Aid costs the US fifteen cents of every $100 of GNP. It's pocket change. Given the commitment to .7 percent, the US annual aid shortfall is $65 billion compared to the $750 billion most Americans fear is given.

In Canada, .3 percent of GNP was allocated to ODA in the Harper government's 2007-2008 budget, down from .34 percent when it took over a year earlier and half the amount allotted two and three decades ago. The ODA figure includes a variety of projects having little to do with poverty reduction in the poorest countries and includes such relatively well-off recipients as Poland, Hungary, Slovenia and the Czech Republic. We can be confident that the number of dollars that ever reaches an actual project or program in an African country is underwhelming.

Even when aid makes it all the way to an African country, and when it's not stolen by corrupt local politicians, it's often used ineffectively. As UNCTAD reports, that's because of the lack of cooperation and coordination among donors and the lack of coherence of their objectives and requirements. This is made worse by their

> failure to reconcile these with the needs, priorities and preferences of the countries receiving assistance. The sheer multiplicity of donors, with different outlooks, accounting systems and priorities have created a landscape of aid that, at best, can only be described as chaotic. This has in turn stretched the

administrative capacities of the recipient [African] countries to breaking point and undermined any pretence of local ownership of development programs. The institutional capacities of the receiving countries have been further weakened by the pressures to reduce the size and functions of the state, a prominent feature of the adjustment programs driven by international finance institutions.[10]

Ludicrous examples abound. Ghana negotiates with twenty-three separate government-to-government donors. Thirty agencies provide aid to Tanzania in 100 projects with 2,500 aid missions a year, and all have separate accounting, financial and reporting systems; the small, overburdened Tanzanian public service produces 2,400 reports a year for its aid donors. When I was in Mozambique years ago as part of an NGO delegation examining Canadian aid projects, I began to think that half of the country's tiny, exhausted public servants spent their days on the road to and from the airport, welcoming and seeing off an endless parade of foreign delegations. The UNCTAD report notes that even the relatively sophisticated civil service of rich countries would have trouble coping with this kind of situation. Yet so long as Western countries treat aid as a political tool to advance their own self-interest, and so long as most international NGOs compete against one another, the prospect of a more rational and less wasteful system remains a pipedream. In the meantime, we criticize Africans for being inefficient.[11]

Chapter 6
The China Factor

The world now understands that China has become a major player in almost every aspect of African life, and that it is bound to have a profound influence on the continent. India, too, is increasing its presence in Africa in important ways, though not with the dramatic profile of the Chinese. The trouble is that it's impossible to predict what the consequences will actually be of China's new role, how much it will change the existing situation, and whether we can expect the impact to be positive or negative. Will Chinese influence help Africa escape its present mess, make things worse, or leave it essentially unchanged? It's too early for anything but speculation.

China became interested in Africa in the years following the 1949 Communist revolution, as African states began winning independence from their colonial masters. Combining revolutionary solidarity with an opportunity to make friends wherever they could, especially in their bitter competition with the Soviet Union, Chinese government officials followed a two-pronged strategy. The Chinese established economic ties with nearly forty African governments between 1956 and 1976 and provided arms and funds to liberation movements in Southern Africa that the Soviet Union wasn't supporting. The most famous single project was the Tanzam railway between Zambia and Tanzania, which the Chinese both funded and actively supervised. It allowed the Zambian government to ship its copper to the world through Tanzania, instead of going through white-ruled Zimbabwe (then Rhodesia) and apartheid South Africa. By the 1980s, however, the Chinese presence in Africa had substantially receded.

Now the Chinese are back with a vengeance. Trade between African countries and China quadrupled to almost $50 billion between 2000 and 2005, making China Africa's third-largest trading partner after the US and the European Union. China is also poised to become the continent's biggest lender, pledging loans of more than $8 billion in 2006 alone. Within a few years, from nowhere China will emerge as the largest foreign player in Africa.

China's main preoccupation is with Africa's raw materials, its natural resources, especially oil, which China desperately needs to drive its roaring economy. But it has quickly diversified into virtually all other significant economic activities. And in what must be seen as a deliberate design of China's rulers, a majority of African countries now receive a share of Chinese investment.

While China has come to Africa to stay, its impact to date is ambiguous. China prides itself on not attaching strings to its deals. It neither demands that African governments introduce particular economic reforms, the way Westerners insist on neoliberal reforms in return for aid and loans, nor demands an end to human rights abuses and corruption, as Westerners occasionally pretend to do. On the one hand, many African governments appreciate this hands-off policy. On the other, among China's closest friends in Africa are the genocidal government of Sudan and the tyrannical government of Zimbabwe. Sudan supplies oil to China in exchange for weapons to be used against the people of Darfur, and China treats Zimbabwe's president Robert Mugabe, friendless outside Africa, as a distinguished statesman. At the Security Council, while all five permanent members have their own reasons not to put serious pressure on the Sudanese government to end its reign of terror in Darfur, the Chinese have led the charge against any serious action being taken. In Zimbabwe, Chinese financial support may be the only thing beyond brute force that keeps the Mugabe government in power.

The problem with this manifestation of China's philosophy of nonintervention is that Africa itself is moving in the opposite direction. There is increasing agreement that African governments should be practicing good governance, democracy, transparency and accountability; without them, it is widely believed, development is all but impossible. A good number of African governments have agreed to undergo reviews by their peers to determine how closely they conform to these standards. Yet just as has been the case with Western governments for the past half-century, Chinese policy is to give active support to governments that practice none of those things and who will never agree to be peer-reviewed. Early in 2007, in an unprecedented show of principle, the African Union denied Sudanese president al-Bashir his proper turn at the rotating presidency of the AU, a symbolic punishment for his deadly war against Darfur. Barely days later, Chinese president Hu Jintao visited Sudan and, among other welcome announcements, presented al-Bashir with an interest-free loan to build a presidential palace. He also called on nations to "respect the sovereignty of Sudan," implicitly criticizing al-Bashir's fellow African rulers. China's disdain for human rights and democracy is a glaring contradiction in the China-Africa equation that may someday have to be resolved.

There are other potential irritants. China supports projects that harm the local environment, as in Gabon and Mozambique, and that have attracted opposition from both African and Western environmental activists. In Zambia, miners accuse a Chinese-owned mine of enforcing inhuman work standards — starvation wages, dangerous conditions, no days off. Chinese immigrants have materialized, in ever-growing numbers, to work in the construction, manufacturing, commercial, extractive and retail industries that China has initiated, prompting charges that Chinese investors are taking jobs rather than creating them. Cheap manufactured goods are flooding African markets, everything from clothing to electronics, damaging not only local African industries but the long-held dream of many African countries to establish an industrial base for their economies. In Ethiopia, for example, the prime minister himself believes 90 percent of the goods available in Addis Ababa's biggest market were made in China. But, he pointed out, affordable products meant Ethiopians could improve their standard of living. That of course presumes that some of the poorest people on earth can afford even inexpensive products.

Late in 2006, an unprecedented China-Africa Forum was held in Beijing, the Chinese capital, attended by forty-eight of Africa's fifty-three countries, including more than forty heads of state. Rarely has a single country ever hosted an entire continent in this manner. At the meeting, Chinese president Hu Jintao made a large number of specific pledges to his African guests. Among them: China would double its assistance to Africa, provide billions in preferential loans, set up a development fund to encourage Chinese companies to invest in Africa, further open China's markets to African exports, train African professionals, and build hospitals throughout Africa. This of course is an enormously attractive list, one that ensures a major role for China for the foreseeable future. Whether Chinese capital can actually lead Africa into a new world of development can't yet be predicted.[1]

Chapter 7
Changing Africa

Things change. Europe and the West have changed, in some ways beyond recognition. In the sixty-odd years since World War II ended, a majority of people in western Europe were able to escape poverty and war for the first time in history. China and India and much of Asia are changing. In the past quarter of a century, hundreds of millions of Asians have escaped poverty for the first time in the history of that region. Africa, too, will change, though it's always been Africa's bad luck that it has no Africa of its own to exploit as Europe and the US developed on the backs of African slaves and African colonies.

What will expedite that change in the right direction? A neat little formula is now widely thrown around by politicians, both Western and African: African solutions for African problems. But it really makes no sense and no one really means it. The links between the West and Africa are so deep and so extensive that for the right kind of change to happen, both "sides" need to be deeply committed. For years, African and Western leaders have had a cynical little deal – African governments would pretend to reform themselves and Westerners would pretend to live up to their pledges and help them.

Certainly Africa must change, by which I mostly mean the behaviors of its political, business and professional elites. And it's reassuring that a certain amount of positive change has already begun. The elites are represented in two continental organizations, both quite new. The first is the African Union (AU, a kind of United Nations for Africa), which far outshines the shoddy record of its predecessor, the Organization of African Unity (OAU), universally derided as the African Dictators' Club. The AU has already plunged into areas that the OAU never had the capacity for, such as sending a military mission to monitor the crisis in Darfur, western Sudan. But its very success also exposes its limitations.

The Darfur mission, like much else on the AU agenda, remains so dependent on the West for resources that its moral authority is significantly lessened. And just as the UN reflects the wild diversity of the entire world, so the AU reflects the vast diversity that is Africa. Just as there's no good reason to expect all 192 members of the UN to agree on many issues, there's little reason to expect the 53 states that constitute the AU to do so. Africa is deeply divided by a series of vexing fault lines — French versus English speakers, north versus south, Christian versus Muslim, South Africa versus Nigeria, democrats versus dictators, terribly poor versus poor — and so by definition is the AU. For these reasons, it will take many years before it plays a truly significant continental role.

In reaction to Western demands, African governments also initiated the New Partnership for Africa's Development (NEPAD), described grandly as "a vision and strategic framework for Africa's renewal." NEPAD's declared role is to assist Africa to attain its development goals by helping to end conflict, promoting good governance among African countries, and promoting regional cooperation and integration. In return for progress in these areas, Africa's leaders expect donor countries to pony up tens of billions of dollars for development purposes. Put positively, the idea is a partnership between Africa and the West. Put less favorably, it still demonstrates Africa's profound reliance on Western funding — unless China takes over some of that role.

But NEPAD's real problem is that there is so much to be done in so many areas that it's difficult to judge progress. Some conflicts have ended, but others, like the near-genocide in Darfur, continue with little sign of resolution. Some states have shown the first signs of democracy, but Zimbabwe and Sudan, to name only two, remain shameful scars. Regional integration and cooperation have been on the African agenda for half a century, as a means to compensate for the destructive breaking-up of the continent into fifty-three states of profoundly different capacities. But while some progress in some parts of the continent has been made, in many others simple cooperation among nations remains a distant goal. NEPAD seems to be most successful at the moment acting like a giant NGO promoting, say, water and sanitation in one country and electrification in another, but without affecting the continent's overall development needs. So far, it seems a frail reed on which to rest the continent's hopes and seems destined to play a secondary role for the foreseeable future.

There is reason for optimism in the increased number of countries that are experiencing a semblance of political democracy. Freedom House, an organization that promotes political rights and civil liberties around the world, defines a free country as one with a democratic political system in which "the government is accountable to its own people, the rule of law prevails, and freedoms of expression, association, belief and respect for the rights of minorities and women are guaranteed." For many years, Freedom House found that a free sub-Saharan African country was a notable exception. In 2006 it found that 70 percent of African countries were either free (11) or partly free (22); 15 countries were deemed not free at all. If this is not yet a glorious result, at least the continent was finally moving in the right direction.

We need both to celebrate this long-awaited development and to be cautious about it. The rights and liberties that constitute democracy are fragile and not to be taken for granted. In many African countries, not only are elections exercises in hypocrisy, but the nature of the democracy leaves much to be desired. Of many examples, including his own country, one Nigerian considers Kenya to be "the worst example of a farcical multi-party democracy, because political parties... depend on the personal ambitions of leaders who own them and can literally do as they please with them. Essentially they rely on... ethnic constituencies, which makes national politics a club of ethnic notables."[1]

Democracy is not just having the right to vote every few years. It must also include a culture of democracy and the apparatus of democracy. Without the entrenchment of the rule of law and human rights, without a commitment to gender equality, an independent judicial system, an army that stays scrupulously out of politics, a free press and free speech, an active civil society, respect for the rights of minorities and for peaceful opponents of the government, no country can be said to be truly democratic. Of course we need to acknowledge that few countries in the world live up to these criteria, whether in the rich, poor or in-between world.

Most exciting, and most hopeful for the future of the continent, are the efforts of Africans themselves. Everywhere across Africa there are civil society groups determined to use these new opportunities to put pressure on governments to rule on behalf of all their citizens, not merely their small group of supporters. NGOs fighting for social justice, democracy, transparent government, gender equality, children's rights, the environment, the rule of law and human rights are well-placed to have a real impact. Many women's groups and AIDS support groups especially play an inspiring and often courageous role. If anyone can forge some African solutions to African problems, it's as likely to be the leaders of civil society as their political leaders.

New technologies have provided tools that add to the strength, creativity and connectedness of civil society.

While travel in Africa is both difficult and expensive, communication is not. Email and the Internet have created links that have not been possible in the past. Out of many small groups emerges a large continent-wide, even worldwide movement. Take *Pambazuka News*, an African-run weekly summary of news and analysis from the continent delivered online at no cost (the editors warmly welcome donations). *Pambazuka News* calls itself an "advocacy tool for social justice" and doesn't pretend to be neutral in the many issues it covers — health, conflict, refugees, education, women, human rights, elections, development, land, freedom of expression. It's an indispensable source of knowledge and connectedness and is seen by almost 100,000 people each week.

Africans are also learning how to deal more effectively with those who really control their destinies. In early 2007, for example, the World Development Movement, a network of NGOs and researchers concerned with poverty issues, published a guide entitled *Building Scrutiny of the World Bank and International Monetary Fund: A Toolkit for Legislators and Those Who Work with Them.* It provides basic information about the international financial institutions (IFIs) and their operations and advice on how national legislators and civil society groups can be more involved in economic policy decisions. As Jeffrey Sachs reminds us, these life-and-death decisions are frequently negotiated between the IFIs and government finance ministries working in isolation.

Creative thinking is going on in other critical areas as well. How does Africa come to grips with its terrible health problems, its inadequate health infrastructures and its crushing brain drain? Increasingly, the answer is seen to lie in breaking away from Western models of specialists, doctors, nurses and large hospitals, and in introducing health care that is appropriate to local resources and capacity. It takes years to graduate a full-fledged doctor or nurse, most of whom prefer to work in cities and then begin to look for much greener pastures — and far higher salaries — in rich countries. But there's an alternative process.

Ordinary people, usually women, and often in rural areas, can be trained to function as community health workers. These people, it is now understood, can be trained to treat the most commonly recurring diseases, teach about sanitation and hygiene, distribute drugs where needed, ensure that daily anti-AIDS drugs are taken regularly, distribute and explain the use of anti-malarial bednets, report more serious illnesses to professionals, and offer the social support that is so often required. What's more, because they lack the formal qualifications needed for a job in the West, these community health workers will remain in their communities, thus dealing with several problems at the same time. These kind of initiatives are quietly being launched across the continent and give real hope for breaking the cycle of poverty and ill health that plagues so much of Africa.

Most African countries also need an unleashed and dynamic private sector. This doesn't mean privatizing all those services and utilities that work most effectively as a public service (and that must be improved as a public service). But at their best, entrepreneurs, whether large or small, run businesses that employ people, make a product that's wanted, and pay taxes to the government. In much of Africa, the best is neither what governments permit nor entrepreneurs attempt. In too many countries, governments have thrown up unnecessary bureaucratic hurdles to running an efficient and profitable business. A former Canadian ambassador to Ethiopia told me he had never known of a single business in the country that did not end up in court, suing the government or taken there by government. This is a certain deterrent to a thriving business sector. For their part, far too many businesspeople treat both the public and the government as a nuisance, if not an enemy, and try to get away with wretched wages and working conditions, a slipshod product and no taxes. It is urgent that this situation change.

Despite the dogmas of the "market fundamentalists," however, the private sector in Africa cannot lead the drive for development. Only governments can provide essential services to all, whether schooling at all levels, proper health care, or justice and equality for women. Civil society and private companies can make important contributions, ideally by being integrated into strong public systems. Neither can be a substitute for government. As in richer countries, only governments can reach the scale necessary to provide services to all their citizens.[2]

Of course many, if not most, African governments still lack the cash and/or the capacity and/or the labor and/or the will to fulfill this role. That's why one of the key functions of civil society is to insist that government commit itself to act on behalf of all citizens. It's the role of both civil society and private companies to support government in this effort.

The Future of the Continent

The four countries with a disproportionate influence on the future development of the entire continent are Nigeria, Ethiopia, the Democratic Republic of Congo (DRC) and South Africa. Together they constitute close to half the population of sub-Saharan Africa and a large majority of its economic strength. Nigeria remains Africa's troubled giant, with vast oil resources, a vibrant population, and problems at every turn. Poverty, corruption and violence are widespread, and in April 2007 a presidential election was widely perceived to be highly undemocratic. Ethiopia, one of the very poorest countries in the world, went to war in 2007 with Somalia on behalf of the United States; it could see an earlier war with neighboring Eritrea re-ignite; and its prime minister, Meles Zenawi, has taken to crushing his opponents. The DRC remains a failed state, and although the new government of Joseph Kabila won a reasonably fair election, his government has little real authority in most of the vast country. Serious conflict continues in several regions. For all three countries, the future is murky. That's why South Africa remains the greatest single hope for the continent.

South Africa's Role

South African businesses are already spreading their modernizing tentacles across Africa, and South African diplomats have intervened in a number of troublesome conflicts. If South Africa can develop successfully, it is seen as the engine that can drive the development of the entire rest of the continent. That is a very big "if." South Africa is a classic case of not knowing whether the glass is half-full or half-empty.

The most impressive fact about the "new South Africa" — the multicolored "rainbow nation" that emerged from apartheid after 1994 — is that it didn't explode into an uncontrollable race-based civil war. White extremists were widely expected not to accept black majority rule. It was the prestige and presence of President Nelson Mandela, more than any other single factor, which persuaded the large majority of whites to give democracy a chance. Still, the legacy of apartheid, both positive and negative, has been profound.

It has proven difficult to reverse the deeply entrenched structures and patterns that evolved over three centuries of white rule and four decades of Afrikaner rule. South Africa is the industrial powerhouse of Africa. Unlike any other country in sub-Saharan Africa, travelers often feel as if they're in a rich, modern country in Europe or North America. The World Economic Forum's *Global Competitiveness Report for 2006-2007* summarizes the problems succinctly: "Although South Africa remains the top economic performer on the continent," it is still suffering from "gross inequalities, high unemployment, major skill shortages and a striking dichotomy between first- and third-world characteristics." Violent crime haunts the country, and while whites and white-owned media are most publicly vocal about it, blacks are the chief victims. Rape of young black girls and women by black men has reached epidemic levels. Large numbers of Africans still live in squalid townships with no clean water, proper sanitation, electricity or acceptable housing.

A new generation of middle class and rich blacks share the amenities and services that have long been available to South Africa's whites. But many blacks lack proper health care and decent schools. Life expectancy has declined since 1994 from fifty-two to forty-five years. This reflects the poor state of Africans' health, since the country's whites have the same life expectancy as in rich countries, close to eighty years.

The South African Institute of Justice and Reconciliation concluded in a recent study that 80 percent of schools — all for blacks — offer education "of such poor quality that they constitute a very significant obstacle to social and economic development."[3] Unemployment has actually increased since 1994 from about one-third to at least 40 percent of all Africans. The HIV/AIDS pandemic continues to play havoc with all aspects of the country's development, and nothing has hurt South Africa more than the incomprehensible refusal of President Thabo Mbeki, Mandela's successor, to take the disease seriously. In addition, Mbeki's government has been touched by several high-profile scandals.

Mbeki has also been reluctant to take the crime epidemic seriously, too often blaming whites for exaggerating the situation. Many white professionals and businesspeople have chosen to emigrate.

On the other hand, South Africa is a functioning democracy. Elections are conducted fairly. The justice system is as impartial as in most Western countries. Mbeki's cabinet is multiracial. The country's resources are abundant. South Africa includes tens of thousands of women and men of all races who are well educated, dynamic, sophisticated and determined to make their country work. There is considerable optimism that adversity can be overcome and that South Africa can play its needed role as the engine that drives the entire continent toward development. For the sake of 800 million Africans, that vision of Africa's future needs to be right.

The Role of Outsiders

Even if sub-Saharan Africa were suddenly transformed into forty-eight peaceful, democratic nations all ready to take the steps necessary for sustainable, equitable development, unless we in the West radically change our role, few positive results can be expected. What the West should now do is obvious: reverse many of its present policies and dogmas. Western governments must say no to the powerful interest groups whose demands are so often destructive to Africa's development.

If the West were serious about "helping" Africa, it would not use the World Trade Organization as a tool of the very richest against the very poorest. It would not insist on private-sector solutions that don't benefit the poor or create employment. It would not dump its surplus food and clothing on African countries. It would not force down the price of African commodities sold on the world market. It would not tolerate tax havens and the massive tax evasion they facilitate. It would not strip Africa of its nonrenewable resources without paying a fair price. It would not continue to drain away some of Africa's best brains. It would not charge prohibitive prices for medicines. In a word, there would be an end to the 101 ways in which rich countries systematically ensure that more wealth pours out of Africa into the West than the West transfers to Africa.

Will China's example promote a new momentum for strong activist governments like itself, even if it is working within a capitalist economic framework? Will the competition between China and the West prove dynamic and constructive or will it become bitter and divisive? China wants to establish military exchanges with African armies, but the United States is actively increasing its military presence and influence throughout the continent, apparently for its antiterrorism project. A good number of Western companies have interests in Africa they by no means intend to surrender. And then there is the likelihood of a greater Indian and Taiwanese presence, leading to both more investments and more complications. Just as at the beginning of the twentieth century it was literally impossible to foresee the eventual end of formal colonialism in Africa and to judge its consequences, so in the early years of the twenty-first century it is impossible to predict the results that new outside influences are bound to have on Africa's future well-being.

This book offers no magic bullets, no easy answers to Africa's problems. There are none. Everywhere you look there are major problems, and all of them must be tackled at the same time, because they all interact. And the tackling must be done by both Africans and outsiders. Africans must change the way their leaders behave and the policies they pursue, and millions are doing just that. And only Westerners can change the way our leaders behave and the policies they pursue, but this task has barely begun. For those who ask "What can I do?" the answer is clear. The most important thing Westerners can do is to make their political and business leaders understand the harm their policies have been causing. Once they acknowledge that an entire new approach to Africa is desperately needed, finding the right policies will come easily.

Who Cares about Africa?

There is no question the rich world can afford to offer Africa the assistance required to build its capacities and to fund the services its citizens so badly need. But the issue is rarely the amount of money available. It's the priorities we assign to that money. It's about political will. It always is.

Despite the evidence, rich countries continue to insist that their interest in Africa is based on compassion, philanthropy and generosity. But all this nobility serves to conceal the real obligation of the rich world — to pay back some of the enormous, incalculable debt we owe Africa. We need to help Africa not out of our selflessness and compassion but as restitution, compensation, an act of justice for the generations of crises, conflict, exploitation and underdevelopment for which we bear so much responsibility. Many speak without irony of the desire to "give something back," without realizing the cruel reality of the phrase. In fact, that's exactly what the rich world should do. We should give back what we've plundered and looted and stolen. Until we think about the West's relationship with Africa honestly, until we face up to the real record, until we acknowledge our vast culpability and complicity in the African mess, until then we'll continue — in our caring and compassionate way — to impose policies that actually make the mess even worse.

In the forty-plus years since my first visit, the dream of a continent that would show the rest of the world new possibilities for the human condition has turned into a grotesque nightmare unimaginable by all save the world's worst racists. In much the same way, the Soviet Union and Mao's China were transformed into egregious perversions of socialism. It was the sin of many of my fellow Western socialists that they refused to acknowledge this reality about the Communist world, that they continued long beyond decency to apologize for some of the most terrible crimes against humanity in human history. It would be unthinkable to make the same mistake now about Africa, to deny the undeniable, to impose a similar brand of political correctness on our thinking about Africa. Then it was in the name of not giving sustenance to the enemies of socialism. Now it's in the name of not giving sustenance to the racists and the many enemies of equality.

Yet dishonesty or rationalization only serves to undermine the fight for equality. The truth is not in doubt. It takes little imagination to look at Africa and see a portrait of unparalleled hopelessness, of a continent that is beyond redemption. It's easy enough to be overwhelmed by despair and a sense of futility. But that's exactly why it's so crucial that the causes for this condition be carefully analyzed and properly understood. For those in the West long committed to Africa, recognizing the source of the crisis is a critical step along the road to reversing it. And reversing it is exactly the job that must be done. The model is the grandmothers across Africa raising their orphaned grandchildren and other vulnerable children — dedicated Africans explaining to us what they need to do the job, and us giving as much of the needed help as we can.

5 million-2.5 million BCE Our ancestors emerge in Ethiopia and eastern Africa

200-700 Rise of the kingdom of Axum and its adoption of Christianity

600-1000 Bantu migration from West and Central Africa to Southern Africa

700-1600 Islam sweeps across North Africa, then moves south of the Sahara

1000-1600 Empires of Ghana, Mali, Songhai, Kanem-Bornu, Zimbabwe, Congo rise and fall

1439 Portuguese explore West African coast

1441 Beginning of African slave trade by Portugal

1562 Britain begins trading Africans as slaves

1650-1850 Height of Atlantic slave trade by Europeans and of Middle East slave trade by Arabs

1652 Dutch establish a colony at the southern tip of Africa, the Cape of Good Hope

1700s Rise of empires of Asante and Dahomey

1807 Britain abolishes slave trade — slavery thrives

1800s Resistance and rebellions by Africans against European interlopers

1800s British and Afrikaners (Dutch) compete for South Africa, wars against local Africans

1818-28 Zulu chief Shaka unites Ngonis against Africans and whites in South Africa

1870-1912 "Scramble for Africa" – height of European imperialism

1870s Zulu wars against British in South Africa

1884-85 Berlin Conference formally divides up Africa among European powers

1899-1902 British-Boer (Afrikaans) war, Britain wins

1920s-30s Birth of anticolonial unrest and of African nationalism

1939-45 World War II accelerates movement for African independence

1948 Nationalist Party, representing Afrikaners, forms government in South Africa

1955-90 Africa becomes pawn in Cold War

1957 Ghana becomes first nation in sub-Saharan Africa to win independence, under Kwame Nkrumah

1958-60 All French colonies in sub-Saharan Africa become independent

1960-64 All British colonies except Rhodesia become independent

1960 Democratic Republic of Congo gains independence from Belgium

1963 Independent African nations form Organization of African Unity (OAU)

1964 Nelson Mandela and fellow freedom-fighters jailed for life in South Africa for resistance to white government

1964-90 Africans in South Africa, Namibia, Rhodesia, Angola and Mozambique form armed liberation movements

1965 White minority government of Rhodesia (Zimbabwe) introduces Unilateral Declaration of Independence from Britain

1966 President Nkrumah of Ghana overthrown by army, first of many army coups across Africa

1967-70 Nigerian Civil War (Biafran War)

1970s-1980s South African white government launches harsh repression against internal opponents and against independent neighbors

1975-2002 Portuguese colonies gain independence — civil wars in Angola and Mozambique backed by Cold War rivals

1980 Rhodesia wins independence after bitter civil war (war of liberation) and becomes Zimbabwe under Robert Mugabe

1980s HIV/AIDS pandemic begins in Africa

1980s World Bank and International Monetary Fund impose Structural Adjustment Programs on most African countries

1986 Nigerian writer Wole Soyinka wins Nobel Prize in Literature
1990 Nelson Mandela and colleagues released from prison
1994 Rwanda's Hutu extremists launch 100 days of genocide against Tutsi minority
1994 Nelson Mandela becomes first democratically elected president of "the new South Africa"
1996 Wars in the Democratic Republic of Congo (also known as Africa's First World War), many African countries involved
2001 African Union replaces discredited OAU; New Partnership for Africa's Development (NEPAD) also begins with mandate to accelerate African development
2003 Conflict in Darfur begins between government of Sudan and Darfur rebels; government and its Janjaweed militias accused of genocide
2005 China begins major push into Africa
2006 Ellen Johnson-Sirleaf elected president of war-torn Liberia, first woman elected president in Africa
2006 Ethiopia invades Somalia — American "war on terror" comes to Africa
2007 Unusually strong rains leading to floods and famines raise fears about the impact of global warming
2007 China's ever-increasing presence in Africa becomes of great concern to Western countries

Notes

Chapter 1. A Diverse Continent, a Common Predicament

1. All references to currency are in US dollars.
2. Jeffrey D. Sachs, *The End of Poverty: Economic Possibilities for Our Time* (New York: Penguin Books, 2005), 256.

Chapter 2. History Matters

1. Hugh Trevor-Roper, *The Rise of Christian Europe* (New York: Macmillan, 1965), 9.
2. Milton Allimadi, "Inventing Africa: New York Times' Archives Reveal a History of Racist Fabrications," *Extra!* Sept./Oct. 2003.
3. Allimadi, "Inventing Africa."
4. Basil Davidson, *Africa in History: Themes and Outlines* (London: Weidenfeld and Nicolson, 1968), 57.
5. Martin Meredith, *The Fate of Africa* (New York: Public Affairs, 2005), 2.
6. Phyllis Johnson and David Martin, *Apartheid Terrorism: A Report on the Devastation of the Frontline States.* Prepared for the Commonwealth Committee of Foreign Ministers on Southern Africa, 1989.
7. Jon Bridgman, *The Revolt of the Hereros* (Berkeley: University of California Press, 2004); Adam Hochschild, *King Leopold's Ghost: A Story of Greed, Terror and Heroism in Colonial Africa* (New York: Mariner Books, 2006).
8. Meredith, *Fate of Africa*, 27.

Chapter 3. Portrait of a Continent

1. Robert Calderisi, *The Trouble with Africa* (New York: Palgrave Macmillan, 2006), 143.
2. Meredith, *Fate of Africa*, 643.

3. Urban Poverty group submission to Commission on Africa, 2004, and UN Habitat, cited by UN News Centre.

4. Fitzhugh Mullan, "Doctors and Soccer Players: African Professionals on the Move," *New England Journal of Medicine*, February 1, 2007.

5. Itai Madamombe, "African Expatriates Look Homeward," *Africa Renewal*, United Nations, October 2006.

6. UNESCO Institute for Statistics, *Global Education Digest*, 2006, "Comparing Educational Statistics Around the World."

7. S. Nock, *Crisis in the Teaching Profession Threatens Education for All*, Global Campaign for Education, 2006.

Chapter 4. The Great Conspiracy

1. Calderisi, *Trouble with Africa*, 77.

2. Meredith, *Fate of Africa*, 379, 386.

3. Meredith, *Fate of Africa*, 307-308.

4. William Easterly, *The White Man's Burden: Why the West's Efforts to Aid the Rest Have Done So Much Ill and So Little Good* (New York: The Penguin Press, 2006), 328.

5. Easterly, *White Man's Burden*, 323.

6. Keith Harmon Snow and David Barouski, "Behind the Numbers, Untold Suffering in the Congo," *ZNET*, March 1, 2006.

7. See also the many reports by the Tax Justice Network, www.taxjustice.net/cms/front_content.php?idcat=53.

8. Nick Mathiason, "Western Bankers and Lawyers Rob Africa of $150 Billion Every Year," *The Observer*, January 21, 2007.

9. Tax Justice Network for Africa, *Looting Africa: Some Facts and Figures*, 2006.

Chapter 5. Western Policies and Africa

1. Jeffrey Sachs, *IMF Can Help to End Shortfalls in Aid that Threaten Death to the Poor*, published online, January 5, 2006.

2. Joseph Stiglitz, *Globalization and Its Discontents* (New York: W.W. Norton, 2002).

3. Sachs, *End of Poverty*, Chapter 10.

4. Eurodad, *Nigeria's Debt Deal Close Up*, December 2006.

5. IRIN News, West Africa, "Criticism of Cotton Subsidies Mounts Ahead of WTO Round," November 29, 2005.

6. *The Lancet*, special reports on "Sexual and Reproductive Health," June 24, November 4, December 2, December 9, 2006.

7. Oxfam, the New Economics Foundation, and the Working Group on Climate Change and Development, *Up in Smoke 2: Report of the Secretariat of the UN Framework Convention on Climate Change*, 2006.

8. Action Aid (UK), *Real Aid 2*, July 5, 2006.

9. Cited in Oxfam and Water Aid, *In the Public Interest: Health, Education, Water and Sanitation for All*, 2006.

10. UNCTAD, *Economic Development in Africa: Doubling Aid*, 2006; see also Easterly, *White Man's Burden*, Chapter 5.

11. UNCTAD, *Economic Development in Africa*.

Chapter 6. The China Factor

1 Firoze Manji and Stephen Marks, eds., *African Perspectives on China in Africa* (Oxford: Fahamu, 2007).

Chapter 7. Changing Africa

1. Tajudeen Abul-Raheem, "Kenya: Who Are Our Enemies and Where Are Our Friends?" *Pambazuka News*, March 22, 2007.

2. Oxfam and Water Aid, *In the Public Interest*.

3. Inter Press Service, "Schooling That Hampers Development," Johannesburg, March 30, 2007.

For Further Information

You can spend a lifetime and still not read a fraction of the books that will help you further understand Africa. The following are some of the ones that seem to me most illuminating of one aspect or another of the African saga.

Anderson, David. *Histories of the Hanged: Britain's Dirty War in Kenya and the End of Empire*. London: Weidenfeld and Nicolson, 2005.

Berkeley, Bill. *The Graves Are Not Yet Full: Tribe and Power in the Heart of Africa*. New York: Basic Books, 2001.

Calderisi, Robert. *The Trouble with Africa*. New York: Palgrave Macmillan, 2006.

Caplan, Gerald. "The Conspiracy Against Africa," *The Walrus*, November 2006.

Caplan, Gerald (for the Organization of African Unity's International Panel of Eminent Personalities on the 1994 Rwandan Genocide). *Rwanda: The Preventable Genocide*. 2000. www.visiontv.ca/RememberRwanda/main_pf.htm.

Davidson, Basil. *Africa in Modern History: The Search for a New Society*. London: Allen Lane, 1978.

Easterley, William. *The White Man's Burden: Why the West's Efforts to Aid the Rest Have Done So Much Ill and So Little Good*. New York: The Penguin Press, 2006.

Fanon, Frantz. *The Wretched of the Earth*. London: Penguin, 1967.

Gourevitch, Philip. *We Wish to Inform You That Tomorrow We Will be Killed With Our Families: Stories from Rwanda*. New York: Farrar, Straus and Giroux, 1998.

Hochschild, Adam. *King Leopold's Ghost: A Story of Greed, Terror and Heroism in Colonial Africa*. London: Macmillan, 1999.

Lewis, Stephen. *Race Against Time*. Toronto: Anansi, 2005.

Maier, Karl. *This House Has Fallen: Midnight in Nigeria*. New York: Public Affairs, 2000.

Mandela, Nelson. *Long Walk to Freedom: The Autobiography of Nelson Mandela*. London: Little, Brown, 1994.

Manji, Firoze and Stephen Marks, eds. *African Perspectives on China in Africa*. Oxford: Fahamu, 2007.

Melvern, Linda. *Conspiracy to Murder: The Rwandan Genocide*. New York: Verso, 2004.

Meredith, Martin. *The Fate of Africa*. New York: Public Affairs, 2005.

Meredith, Martin. *Robert Mugabe: Power, Plunder and Tyranny in Zimbabwe*. Johannesburg: Jonathan Ball, 2002.

Nzongola-Ntalaja, Georges. *The Congo from Leopold to Kabila: A People's History*. London: Zed, 2002.

Oliver, R. and J. Fage. *A Short History of Africa*. London: Penguin, 1988.

Peterson, Scott. *Me Against My Brother: At War in Somalia, Sudan and Rwanda*. London: Routledge, 2001.

Poku, N. and A. Whiteside, eds. *The Political Economy of AIDS in Africa*. Aldershot: Ashgate, 2004.

Rodney, Walter. *How Europe Underdeveloped Africa*. Washington, DC: Howard University Press, 1973.

Sachs, Jeffery D. *The End of Poverty*. New York: Penguin Books, 2005.

Stiglitz, Joseph. *Globalization and Its Discontents*. New York: Norton, 2002.

Theroux, Paul. *Dark Star Safari: Overland from Cairo to Cape Town*. London: Hamish Hamilton, 2002.

Wrong, Michela. *In the Footsteps of Mr. Kurtz: Living on the Brink of Disaster in the Congo*. London: Fourth Estate, 2000.

Websites

Thanks to the Internet, it is possible to follow and understand events in Africa relatively closely. Of many hundreds of sites, these are the ones I most rely on:

BBC: news.bbc.co.uk./hi/English/world/Africa
The best regular coverage of Africa by a mainstream medium.

IRIN: www.irinnews.org/IRIN-Africa.aspx
A service of the United Nations.

Pambazuka News: www.pambazuka.org
Weekly news and analysis from a social justice perspective.

ZNet Africa Watch: www.zmag.org/RaceWatch/africawatch.cfm

In addition, most large NGOs have websites that carry news and analysis of African life, society, economics and politics.

Acknowledgments

As always, my first thanks go to my wife Carol Phillips, without whom…

Then:

Thanks to Ken Alexander, editor of the *Walrus*, for publishing the essay from which this book springs.

Thanks to Patsy Aldana, publisher of Groundwood Books, for believing that what I had to say merited a Groundwork Guide.

Thanks to managing editor Nan Froman and designer Michael Solomon at Groundwood for their excellent collaboration.

And thanks to Leon Grek, Deborah Viets and Lloyd Davis for their meticulous work on maps and charts, copyediting and indexing, respectively.

Above all, thanks to Jane Springer, an editing genius who also knows a great deal about Africa. This book is much richer for her suggestions.

Index

abortion, 41, 96
Africa
  ancient, 15, 16–17, 129
  colonial, 19–33, 129–30
  difference between
      northern and sub-
      Saharan, 8–9
  "discovery" of, 13
  diversity, 8–10, 114–15
  divided among European
      powers, 19–21, 22
  ethnic ties reinforced by
      partition, 25–29, 78
  history, 13–36, 129–31
  influence of Western
      policies over, 83–107
  quality of life in colonial
      era, 29–30
  underdevelopment,
      10–11, 33, 38–39
African National Congress,
  32
African Union, 111, 114
agriculture
  threatened by climate
      change, 99–100
  threatened by imported
      produce, 93, 94–95
AIDS (and HIV), 75, 83
  civil society groups try to
      deal with, 117
  drugs to combat, 101,
      119
  health-care professionals
      killed by, 50
  lack of retroviral drugs
      for children, 101
  prevalence in rural
      regions, 40
  prevalence of HIV, 45
  prevention programs,
      63–65, 96–98
  sex with virgins believed
      to cure, 42
  social and economic
      costs, 45–47, 52, 62,
      69
  South Africa interferes
      with attempts to deal

  with, 63–65, 123
  statistics, 45, 46, 69
America's Tyrant (Kelly), 72
Amin, Idi, 63, 70
Angola
  civil war, 21, 73–75, 130
  as failed state, 68
  governed by Europeans,
      23, 25–26
  leftist government
      opposed by US, 70
  liberation movement,
      34–35
  racist regime backed by
      Western nations, 70
  raided by South Africa,
      22
apartheid, 37–38, 89, 109
  backed by Western
      governments, 70, 74
  history, 31–32
  legacy, 122–23
  protests met with deeper
      oppression, 35
  role in destabilizing
      South Africa's
      neighbors, 21–22
al-Bashir, Omar, 111
Belgian Congo. See Congo,
  Democratic Republic of
  (DRC)
Belgium
  atrocities committed in
      Africa, 23–25
  and independence of
      Congo, 29, 130
  opposes UN resolution
      for African
      independence, 34
  productivity compared
      with that of much of
      Africa, 39
  role in death of
      Lumumba, 70, 72
  role in Rwandan
      genocide, 16, 70, 78
  sponsorship of "Big
      Men," 69–72

Benin, 63, 95
"Big Men," 59–76
Blair Commission on
  Africa, 103
Bokassa, Jean-Bédel, 24,
  62–63, 71–72
Bongo, Omar, 64, 66
Botswana, 22, 46, 62, 69
brain drain, 47–52, 118–19,
  124
Britain. See United
  Kingdom
Burundi, 68, 79
Bush, George H.W., 73
Bush, George W., 89,
  96–98, 105–6

Canada
  attracts professionals
      from Africa, 50–51
  availability of doctors,
      49, 50
  citizens boycott South
      African products, 32
  foreign aid, 103, 105–7
  grandparents support
      African counterparts,
      57
  health-care budget, 47
  mines owned by
      Canadian companies,
      75–76
  capital flight, 81–82, 89,
      91
Catholic Church, 70, 78, 80
Central African Republic,
  24, 62–63, 68, 71–72
Chad, 68, 70, 95
Cheney, Dick, 74
children
  diseases most likely to
      kill, 44–46
  enrolment in primary
      school, 53
  prevalence of AIDS, 46
China
  aid to Africa, 109–10,
      115, 125, 131
  complicity in Darfur

genocide, 71,
110–111
goods flood African
markets, 111–12
refusal to take global
warming seriously,
98–99
trade with Africa, 108–9,
111–12, 125, 131
working conditions in
Chinese-owned mines,
111
China-Africa Forum, 112
Christian Aid, 94, 99
cities, 42–44
civil society groups, 117–18
civil wars, 21–22, 23,
68–69, 75, 130, 131
climate change, 98–100
Clinton, Bill, 80
colonialism, 16, 19–33
rebellions against colonial
powers, 27, 30, 35
Communism, 63, 70–71,
72–75, 108–9
community health workers,
119
"conditionalities," 56,
86–87, 94, 109–10
condoms, 46, 97–98
Congo, Democratic
Republic of (DRC), 8,
121, 130
atrocities under Belgian
King Leopold, 23–25
civil war, 75, 131
debt, 89
education in, 29
gold smuggled out of,
75–76
health-care budget, 47
murder of Lumumba,
70, 72
sale of natural resources,
100
Congo-Brazzaville, 68
Congress of Berlin, 19–21,
129
Conté, Lansana, 68
contraception, 41
corruption, 66, 76–82, 92,
100
cotton, 94–96

coups, 67, 130

Dallaire, Roméo, 79–80
Dar es Salaam, Tanzania, 42
Darfur, 71, 84, 110, 111,
114, 131
Davidson, Basil, 17
de Klerk, F.W., 32
debt, 88–91
debt relief, 89–90, 103
democracy, 32, 36, 62, 115,
116
Democratic Republic of
Congo. See Congo,
Democratic Republic
of (DRC); Zaire
Denmark, foreign aid, 105
dictatorship, 22, 24, 28,
61–63, 65, 70–71, 72
disease, 44–47
doctors, shortage of, 48–50,
55

economic inequality, 37–38,
65, 122–23. See also
poverty
education, 29–30, 87
of women, 41, 52–58,
53. See also brain drain
Eisenhower, Dwight, 72
elections
legitimacy of, 28, 31, 62,
116–17
South African, 31, 32,
36, 124
entrepreneurs, 119–20
environment, 98–100, 111
Eritrea, 67–68, 121
Ethiopia, 8, 64, 121
Chinese imports flood
market, 111–12
debt, 89, 90
economic inequality, 38
evidence of prehistoric
humans found in, 4,
129
health-care budget, 47
invasion of Somalia, 67,
121, 131
military regime
supported by Soviet
Union, 70–71
pre-colonial civilization,

17
resistance to against
colonial powers, 27
shortage of doctors, 49
slaughter of people by
Italians, 23
threatened by climate
change, 99–100
war with Eritrea, 67–68
Europe
Africans perceived as
inferior race by,
18–19, 23–25
economic impact of slave
trade, 19. See also
colonialism
European Union (EU)
agricultural subsidies
threaten African
farmers, 93
obstructs access to
generic drugs, 101–2

faith-based policies, 96–98
family planning, 41, 96
Ferguson, Niall, 22
Ford, Gerald, 74
foreign aid, 102–7
bureaucracy related to,
106–7
"phantom" aid, 104–5
"tied," 103–4
foreign direct investment,
91–92
forestry industry, 100
France
access to doctors, 49
atrocities committed in
colonies, 22–23, 30
complicity in African
government
corruption, 82
complicity in Rwandan
genocide, 16, 70, 75,
79–80, 86
destruction of
government property
in Guinea, 30
failure to build
universities in
colonies, 29
opposes UN resolution
for African

independence, 34
"phantom" foreign aid,
    104–5
relations with former
    colonies, 85–86
sponsorship of "Big
    Men," 69, 70, 71–72
free trade, 93–96
Freedom House, 116

Gabon, 66, 111
Gambia, 62
gender inequality, 40–42,
    46
generic drugs, 102
genocide, 14–16, 23–24,
    70, 71, 75
Germany
    colonization of Rwanda,
        21, 78
    foreign aid, 105
    genocide in Namibia,
        23–24
Ghana, 8
    bureaucracy involved in
        receiving foreign aid,
        107
    cotton industry
        threatened, 94–95
    coup, 130
    doctor shortage, 49
    doctors and nurses
        emigrate to West,
        50–51
    gains independence, 34
    poultry industry
        threatened by imports,
        94
    precolonial civilization,
        27
    underdevelopment, 10
Giscard d'Estaing, Valery,
    71–72
governments
    failure of, 68
    heads of state, 61–66
    as impediments to
        entrepreneurs, 120
    indebtedness, 88–91
    overthrown, 67
    peer review of, 110–11
    theft of money by,
        57–58, 72, 77–81. See

also dictatorship;
    elections;
        monarchy
grandmothers, as activists,
    57, 128
Guinea, 30, 63, 68, 95

Habyarimana, Juvénal,
    78–79
heads of state, 61–66
    overthrown, 66–67, 130
health care, 118–19
    fees for, 87
    shortage of doctors and
        nurses, 48–51, 55
    spending on, 47
health research, 100–102
Heritage Foundation, 74
history, distortion of,
    13–14, 16–17
HIV/AIDS. See AIDS
Holland, foreign aid, 105
How Europe
    Underdeveloped Africa
    (Rodney), 33
Hu Jintao, 111, 112

imperialism, 84–86
independence, 22, 28–36,
    130
betrayal by "Big Men,"
    59–61
India, 38, 108, 125
informal economy, 43
International Development
    Research Centre (IDRC),
    51
International Labor
    Organization (ILO), 44
International Monetary
    Fund (IMF), 52, 55–58,
    72, 84–85, 86–87,
    130
International Planned
    Parenthood Federation,
    96
Internet, 55, 118

Johnson-Sirleaf, Ellen, 131

Kabila, Joseph, 121
Kaunda, Kenneth, 34
Kelly, Sean, 72

Kenya
    corruption of Moi
        government, 77
    debt, 89
    education in, 56–58
    family planning facilities
        closed, 96
    land expropriated by
        Britain, 23
    Mau Mau uprising, 30
    nature of democracy,
        116–17
Kibaki, Mwai, 56–58
Kirkpatrick, Jeane, 74
Kissinger, Henry, 74–75

Lalibela, Ethiopia, 17
Lancet, 97–98
Lastman, Mel, 16
Leopold (king of Belgium),
    23, 24
Lesotho, 22, 46, 69
Lewis, Stephen, 57
Liberia, 68, 89, 131
life expectancy, 29, 41, 46
literacy, 29–30, 41
Livingstone, David, 13
Lord's Resistance Army, 68,
    71
Lumumba, Patrice, 70,
    72–73

Madagascar, 23, 30
Malawi, 46, 50, 65–66, 89
Mandela, Nelson, 32,
    35–36, 74, 122, 130,
    131
"market fundamentalism,"
    86–87, 120–21
Marxism, 63, 70–71
Mbeki, Thabo, 63–65,
    123–24
media, 14–16
Meredith, Martin, 39, 62
mining industry, 75–76,
    91–92, 100, 109
Mitterrand, François, 80
Mobutu, Joseph (Mobutu
    Sese Seko), 63, 70,
    72–73
Moi, Daniel arap, 77
Mozambique
    civil war, 21–22

cruelty of Portuguese
colonizers, 23, 30
debt, 90
environmental concerns,
111
foreign aid undermined,
104–5, 107
governed by Europeans,
25–26
liberation movement,
34–35, 130
life expectancy, 46
public servants' lack of
higher education, 54
racist regime backed by
Western nations, 70
raided by South Africa,
22
rebels armed by Western
nations, 70
Mswati III (king of
Swaziland), 65
Mugabe, Robert, 61, 64–65,
71, 110, 130
Museveni, Yoweri, 66, 71
Mutharika, Bingu wa,
65–66

Namibia, 21–24, 46, 130
national sovereignty, 84–86
natural resources, 37,
59–60, 72–73, 109. *See
also* forestry industry;
mining industry;
oil industry
neocolonialism, 84–86
neoliberalism, 86–87
New Partnership for Africa's
Development (NEPAD),
115–16
New York Times, 14
Niger, 90
Nigeria, 8, 121
civil war, 130
cotton industry
threatened, 95
debt cancellation deal,
89–90
doctor shortage, 49
doctors emigrating to
US, 50
economic inequality, 71,
92

governed indirectly by
Europeans, 26–27
health-care budget, 47
Obasanjo's attempt at
third term, 66
political unrest, 68–69
racist depiction of, 14
theft of oil revenues by
government, 77
Nkrumah, Kwame, 34
North Africa, difference
from sub-Saharan Africa,
8–9
Norway, foreign aid, 49,
105
nurses, shortage of, 50
Nyerere, Julius, 34, 64

Obasanjo, Olusegun, 66
official development
assistance (ODA). *See*
foreign aid
oil industry, 71, 91–92
Organization of African
Unity (OAU), 114, 130

Pambazuka News, 118
pharmaceutical industry,
100–102
political parties
legitimacy of, 116–17
organized along ethnic
lines, 28
in South Africa, 31, 32
Portugal, 129–30
atrocities committed in
colonies, 22–23
destruction of
Mozambique
infrastructure, 30
opposes UN resolution
for African
independence, 34
settler states, 25–26
sponsorship of "Big
Men," 69–70
poverty
Africa's inability to
escape, 11, 38
and corruption, 76–82
and "phantom aid,"
103–4
dealing with more

effectively, 118–19
reduction programs, 87
in rural regions, 39–40
urban, 42–44
of women and girls, 46
Poverty Reduction Strategy
Papers, 87
public services, privatization
of, 86–87, 120–21

racism, 13–18, 23–25
Reagan, Ronald, 74
Rhodesia
civil war, 130
liberation movement,
34–35, 130
racism of British
colonizers, 24–25
resistance to colonizers,
27
as settler state, 25–26
Western nations support
racist regime, 70. *See
also* Zambia;
Zimbabwe
Rodney, Walter, 33
rural regions, 39–40
Rwanda
colonized by Germany,
21
debt, 88–89
doctor shortage, 49
genocide, 14–16, 70,
78–80, 86, 131
health-care budget, 47
involvement in Congo
war, 68, 75
life expectancy, 46
women in Parliament, 40

Sachs, Jeffrey, 11, 84–85,
86, 118
safe sex, 97–98
Salisbury, Lord, 21
Savimbi, Jonas, 73–74
Senegal, 62
settler states, 25–26
sex trade, 46, 98
sexual abstinence, 46,
97–98
Sierra Leone, 23, 68
slavery, 17–19, 31, 113, 129
slums, 38, 43

Smith, Ian, 70
Smith, Patrick, 81–82
Somalia
    death of US soldiers, 80
    dictatorship, 70
    invaded by Ethiopia, 67,
        121, 131
South Africa, 8
    apartheid, 21–22, 31–32,
        70, 74, 109
    atrocities committed
        by colonizers, 23
    attracts professionals
        from other African
        nations, 50
    debt, 89
    denied funding for sexual
        and reproductive
        health programs,
        96
    destabilization of
        neighbors, 21–22, 130
    economic inequality,
        122–23
    education in, 53, 54
    elections, 31, 32, 36
    as example for other
        African nations,
        121–24
    foreign investment, 91
    independence, 21
    liberation movement,
        34–35
    life expectancy, 46
    Mandela released from
        prison, 35–36
    racism of colonizers, 25
    refusal to deal with
        AIDS, 63–67, 123
    resistance against
        colonization, 27, 129
    threatened by AIDS, 69,
        123
South African Institute of
    Justice and
    Reconciliation, 123
South Korea, 10
South West Africa. See
    Namibia
Soviet Union, 69–71,
    73–74, 108–9
Soyinka, Wole, 61, 68, 131
Stanley, Henry, 16

Stephen Lewis Foundation,
    57
Stiglitz, Joseph, 86
Structural Adjustment
    Programs (SAPs), 87,
    130
Sudan
    atrocities in Darfur, 68,
        71, 84, 110, 111, 114,
        131
    al-Bashir denied African
        Union presidency, 111
    debt, 89
    dictatorship, 71, 115
    pre-colonial civilization,
        17
    relations with China,
        110–115
Swaziland
    economic inequality, 65
    life expectancy, 46
    prevalence of HIV, 65
    shortage of nurses, 50
    threatened by AIDS, 69
Sweden, foreign aid, 105

Taiwan, 125
Tanzam railway, 109
Tanzania, 21
    bureaucracy related to
        foreign aid, 107
    gains independence, 34
    life expectancy, 46
    Tanzam railway, 109
    urban poverty, 42
Tarzan, 13
Touré, Amadou Toumani,
    95–96
trade, 93–96
Transparency International,
    82
Trevor-Roper, Hugh, 13–14
tuition fees, 56, 87
2005 World Wealth Report,
    37–38

Uganda
    debt, 89, 90
    health-care budget, 47
    internal conflict, 68, 71
    involvement in Congo
        war, 75
    life expectancy, 46

Museveni rewrites
    constitution to retain
    power, 66, 71
Museveni sponsored by
    Western nations, 66,
    71
ruled by Idi Amin, 63,
    70
shortage of doctors, 49
shortage of nurses, 50
smuggling of gold out of
    Congo, 75–76
and Tutsi invasion of
    Rwanda, 78
unemployment, 43–44,
    123
United Kingdom
    Africans serve in military
        during World War II,
        25
    atrocities committed in
        colonies, 22–23
    attracts professionals
        from Africa, 50–51
    availability of doctors, 49
    economic effect of slave
        trade, 19
    foreign aid, 105
    mines owned by British
        companies, 75–76
    opposes UN resolution
        for African
        independence, 34
    on partition of Africa, 21
    resistance against colonial
        rule of, 27, 30, 129
    settler states, 25–27
    sponsorship of apartheid,
        70
    sponsorship of "Big
        Men," 69, 70, 71
    struggle with Dutch for
        control of South
        Africa, 31, 129
United Nations Population
    Fund (UNFPA), 96
United Nations (UN)
    denunciation of
        apartheid, 32
    General Assembly calls
        for independence of
        African colonies,
        34

Human Development
  Index, 10
mission in Rwanda,
  79–80
United States
  agricultural subsidies
    threaten African
    farmers, 94–95
  attracts professionals
    from Africa, 50–51
  availability of doctors,
    49, 50
  development aided by
    slavery, 18, 19, 113
  faith-based family
    planning programs,
    96–98
  foreign aid, 95, 103–4,
    105–6
  health-care budget, 47
  hinders UN mission in
    Rwanda, 80
  investment in mines by
    US companies, 91–92
  obstructs access to
    generic drugs, 101–2
  opposes UN resolution
    for African
    independence, 34
  orders murder of
    Lumumba, 70, 72
  sponsorship of apartheid,
    70, 74
  sponsorship of "Big
    Men," 69–72, 74–75
universities, 29, 54–55
USSR. See Soviet Union

wars, 67–68, 121, 131
  civil wars, 21–22, 23,
    68–69, 75, 130, 131
Washington Consensus, 87,
  130
Western nations
  complicity in genocide,
    16, 78–80
  complicity in
    government
    corruption, 77–82
  complicity with African
    tyrants, 59–61, 69–76
  dependence on slave
    trade, 19

emigration of African
  doctors to, 48–51
farm subsidies, 93,
  94–95
foreign aid, 102–7
G8 summits, 88
influence of policies over
  Africa, 83–107,
  124–26
role in
  underdevelopment of
  Africa, 11, 33
women
  education of, 41, 53
  prevalence of AIDS
    among, 46
  rights of, 40–42, 46
  in Rwandan Parliament,
    40
  sexual abuse of, 97
World Bank, 52, 55–58, 70,
  72, 84, 86–87, 100, 130
World Development
  Movement, 118
World Economic Forum,
  122–23
World Health Organization
  (WHO), 48–50
World Trade Organization
  (WTO), 93, 95
World Wildlife Foundation,
  100

Zaire
  governed by Mobutu, 63,
    64, 72–73
  Western sponsorship of
    Mobutu, 70, 72, 75.
  See also Congo,
    Democratic Republic
    of (DRC)
Zambia, 8, 21
  debt, 90
  gains independence, 34
  labor standards in
    Chinese-owned mine,
    111
  life expectancy, 46
  Lozi elite cooperates with
    colonizers, 27–28
  racist regime sponsored
    by Western nations,
    70

raided by South Africa,
  22
Tanzam railway, 109
threatened by AIDS, 69
Zenawi, Meles, 121
Zimbabwe
  civil war, 130
  governed by Mugabe, 64,
    65, 71, 110, 115
  independence, 22, 35,
    130
  life expectancy, 46
  pre-colonial civilization,
    17, 129
  raided by South Africa,
    22
  relations with China, 110
  resistance against
    colonizers, 35